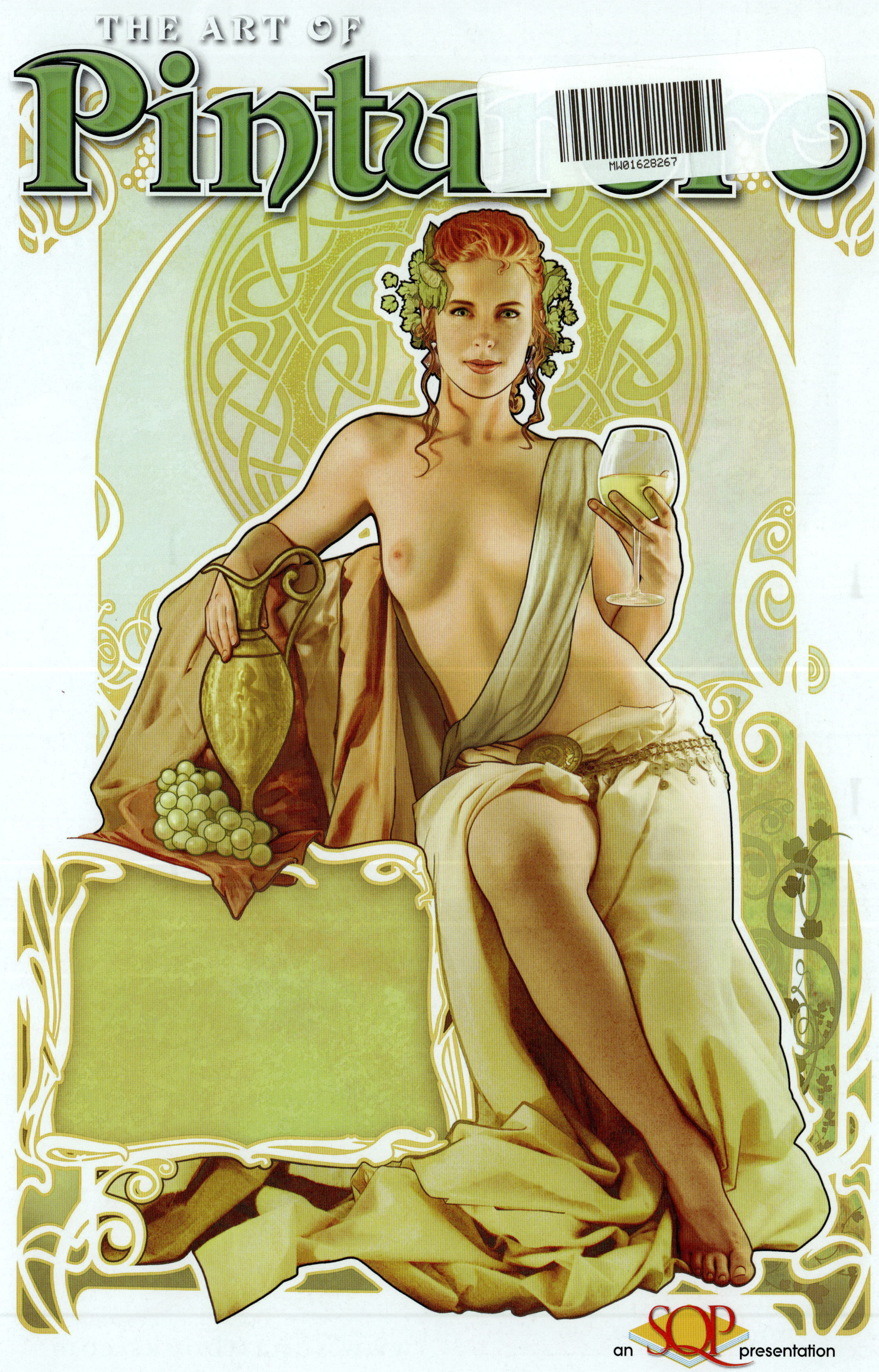
THE ART OF
Pintu
an SQP presentation

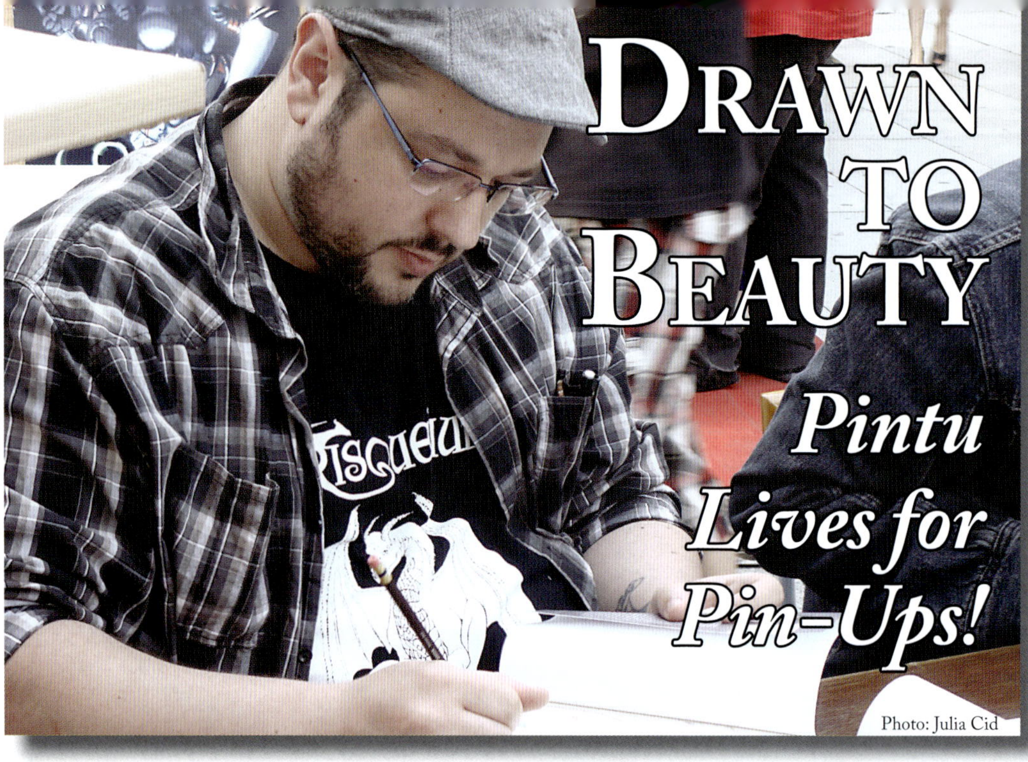

Drawn to Beauty

Pintu Lives for Pin-Ups!

Photo: Julia Cid

Born in Madrid, Spain in 1975, the artist known as Pinturero began his career learning at the Higher School of Professional Drawing (ESDIP), in Madrid. There he graduated to instructor, teaching the finer points of airbrushing and illustration techniques until 2001.

Seeking a career as a freelancer, Pintu quickly found steady and well-received assignments in varied fields: editorial illustration, mural painting, pre-production for animation, working alone or in a group. While advertising is where he is most experienced. it's in the world of the pin-up that he finds the most "reward". This collection of his hand-picked favorites will showcase that ability.

As a cover artist he has attained an international following, showcasing his works in Spain, Italy, the UK and the United States, proving once again that pin-up art needs no translation!

Pintu currently lives in Corunna City, sharing space with other illustrators in the Baobab Study (baobabestudio.blogspot.com).

www.pinturero.com

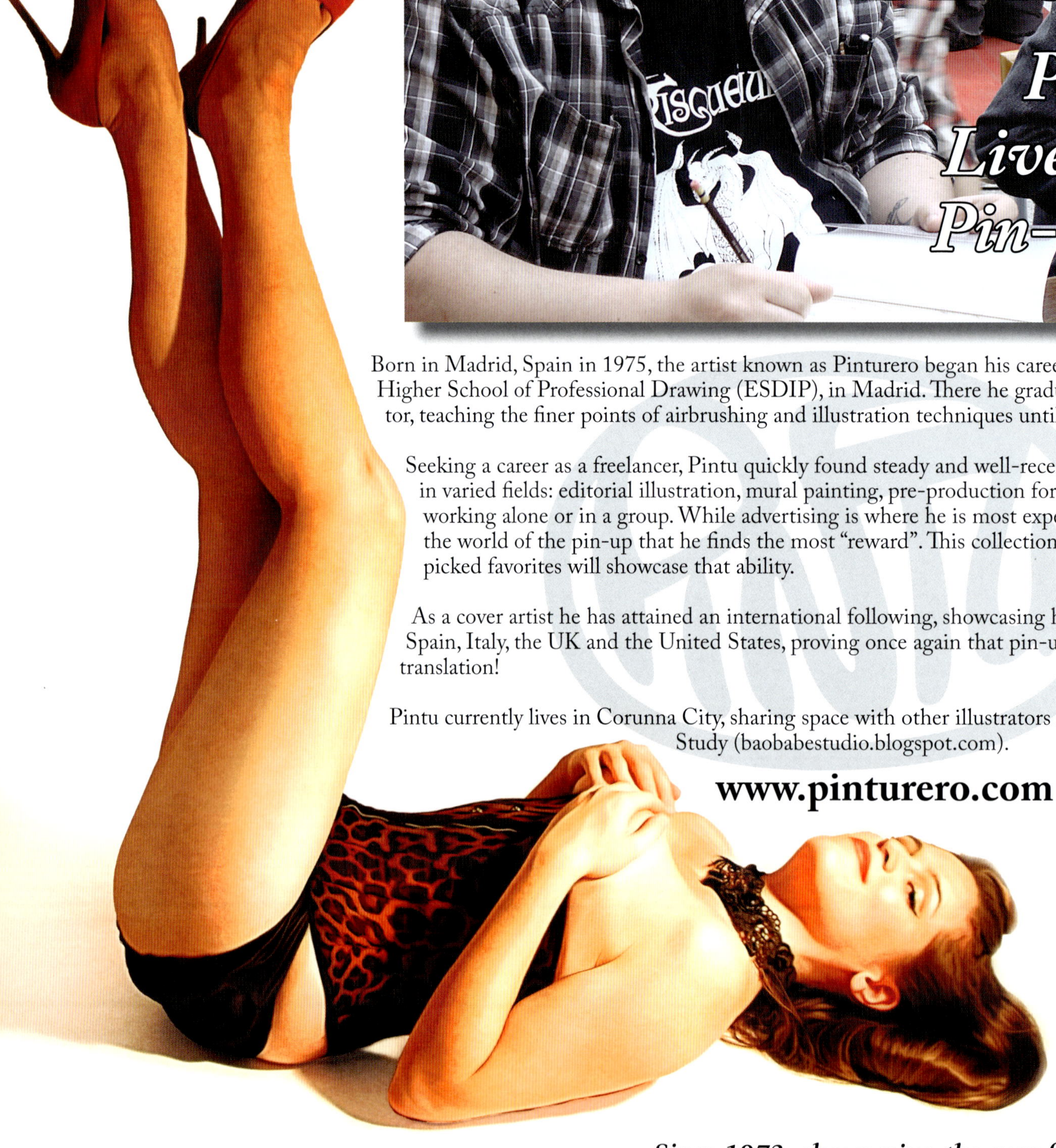

Since 1973, showcasing the very finest in fantasy, erotic, & pin-up illustration.

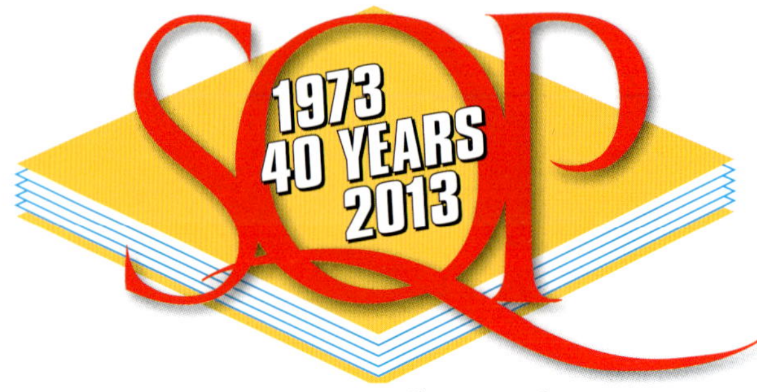

www.sqpartbooks.com

The Art of Pinturero

Book design by Grassy Knoll Studios.

Published by SQP Inc.
PO Box 248 - Columbus NJ 08022

Sal Quartuccio & Bob Keenan - Publishers

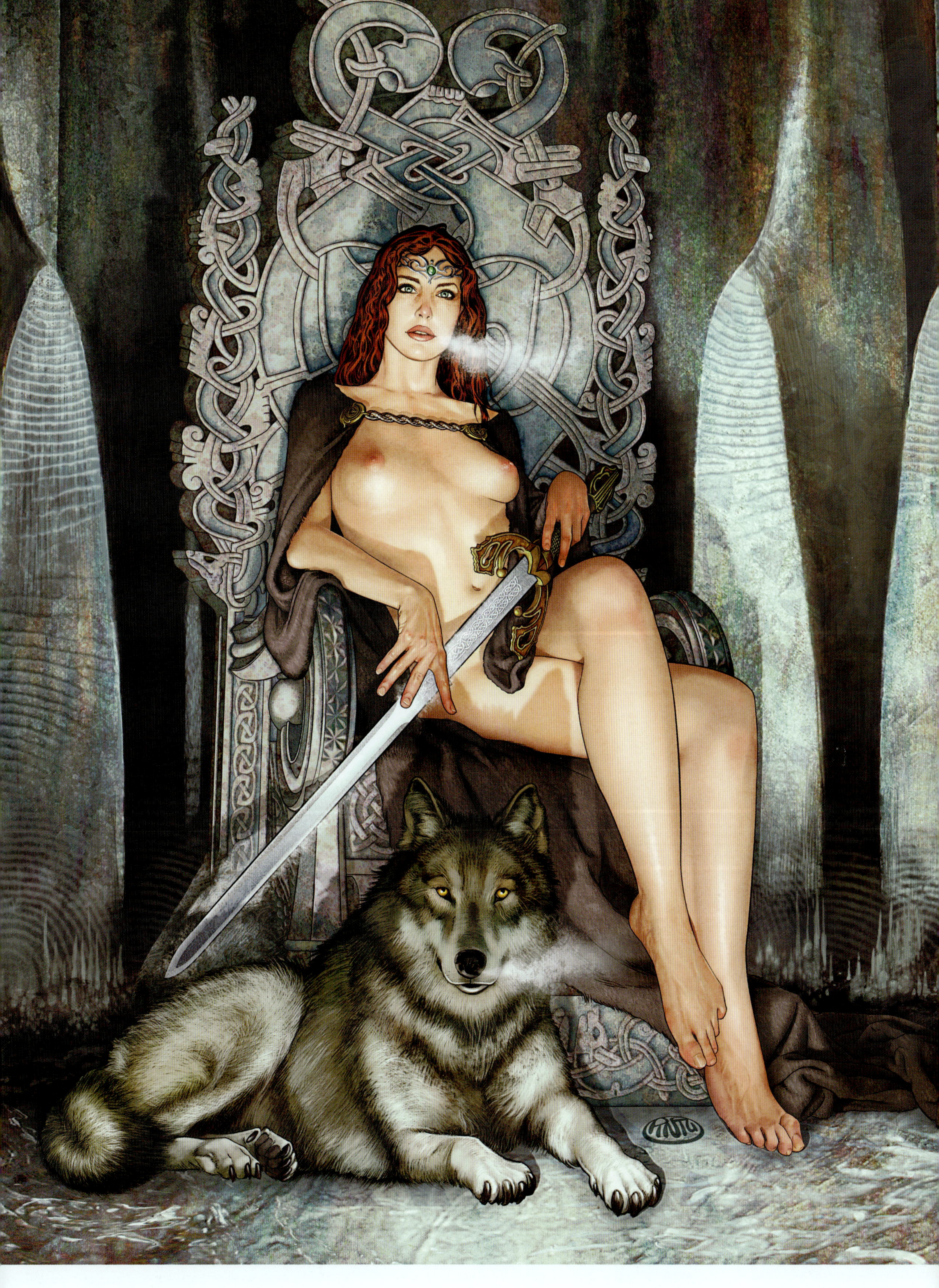

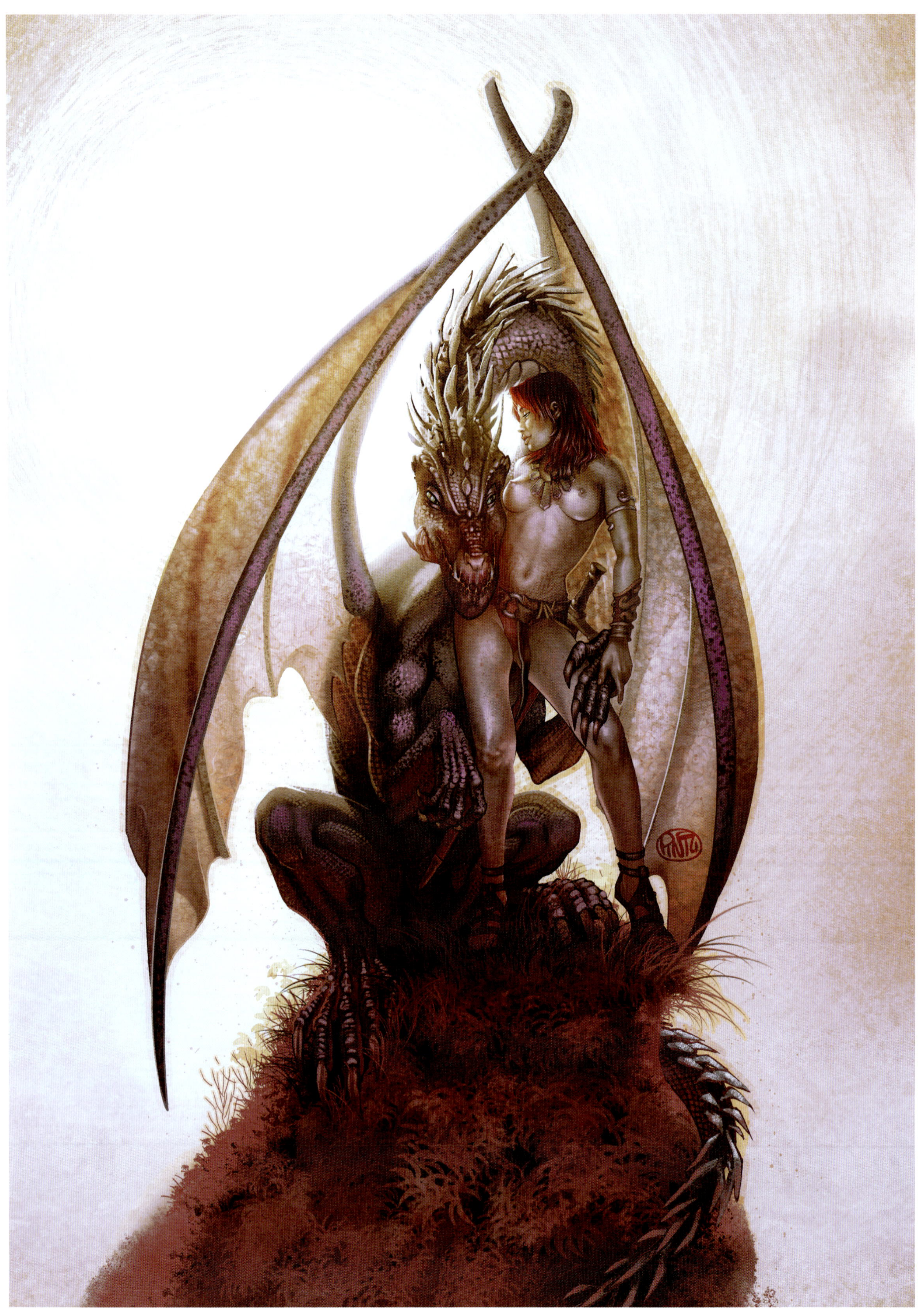

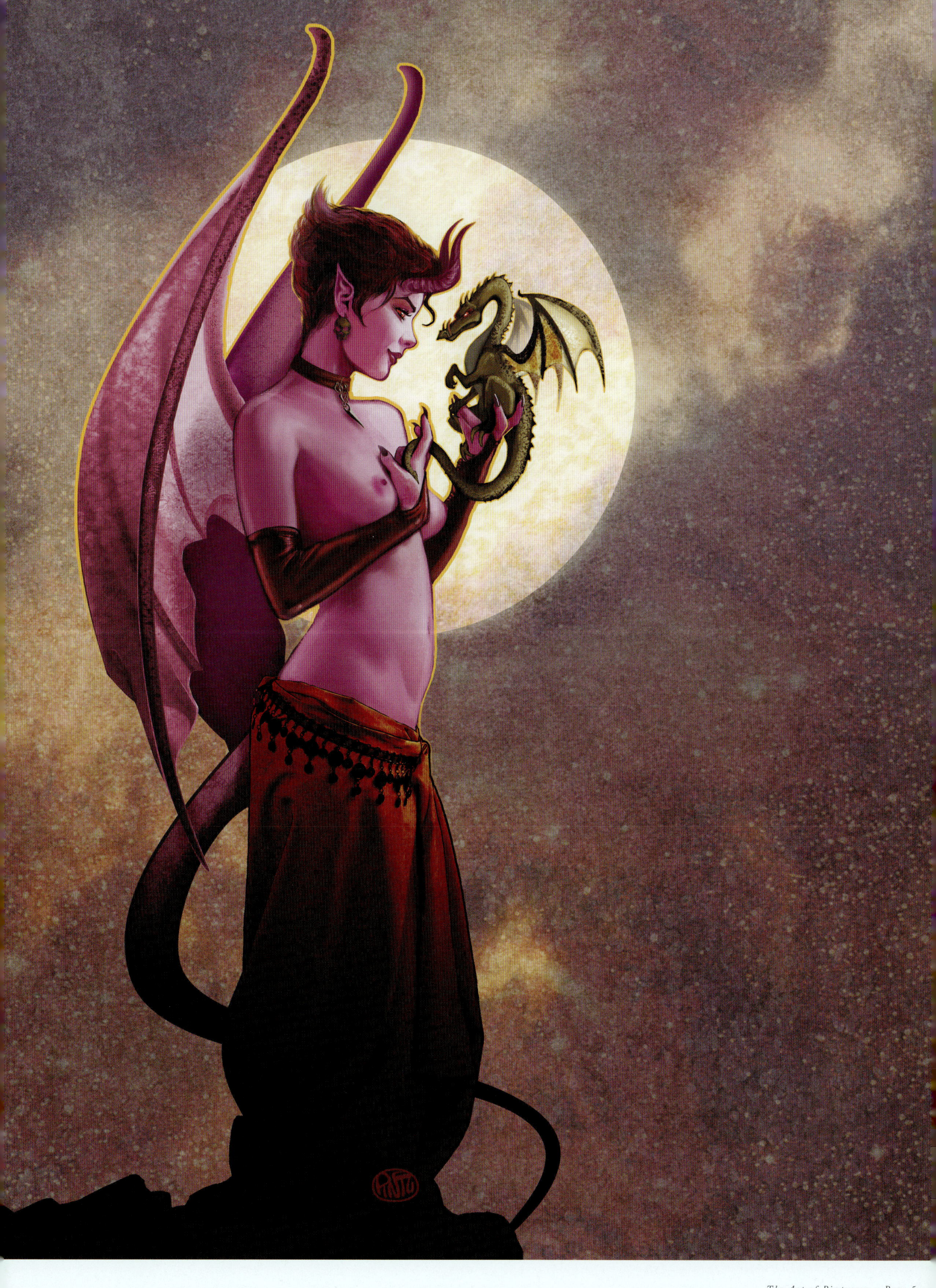

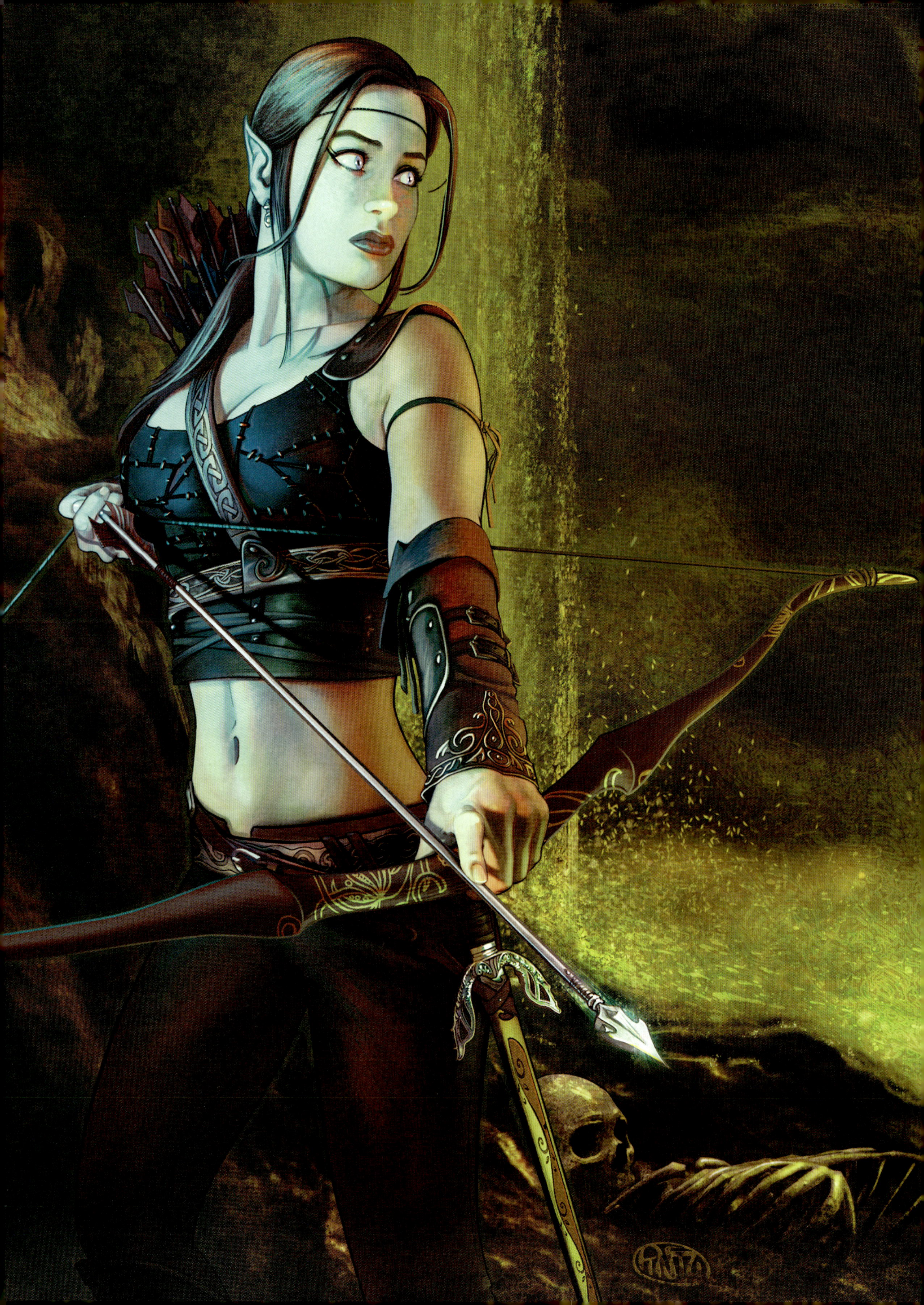

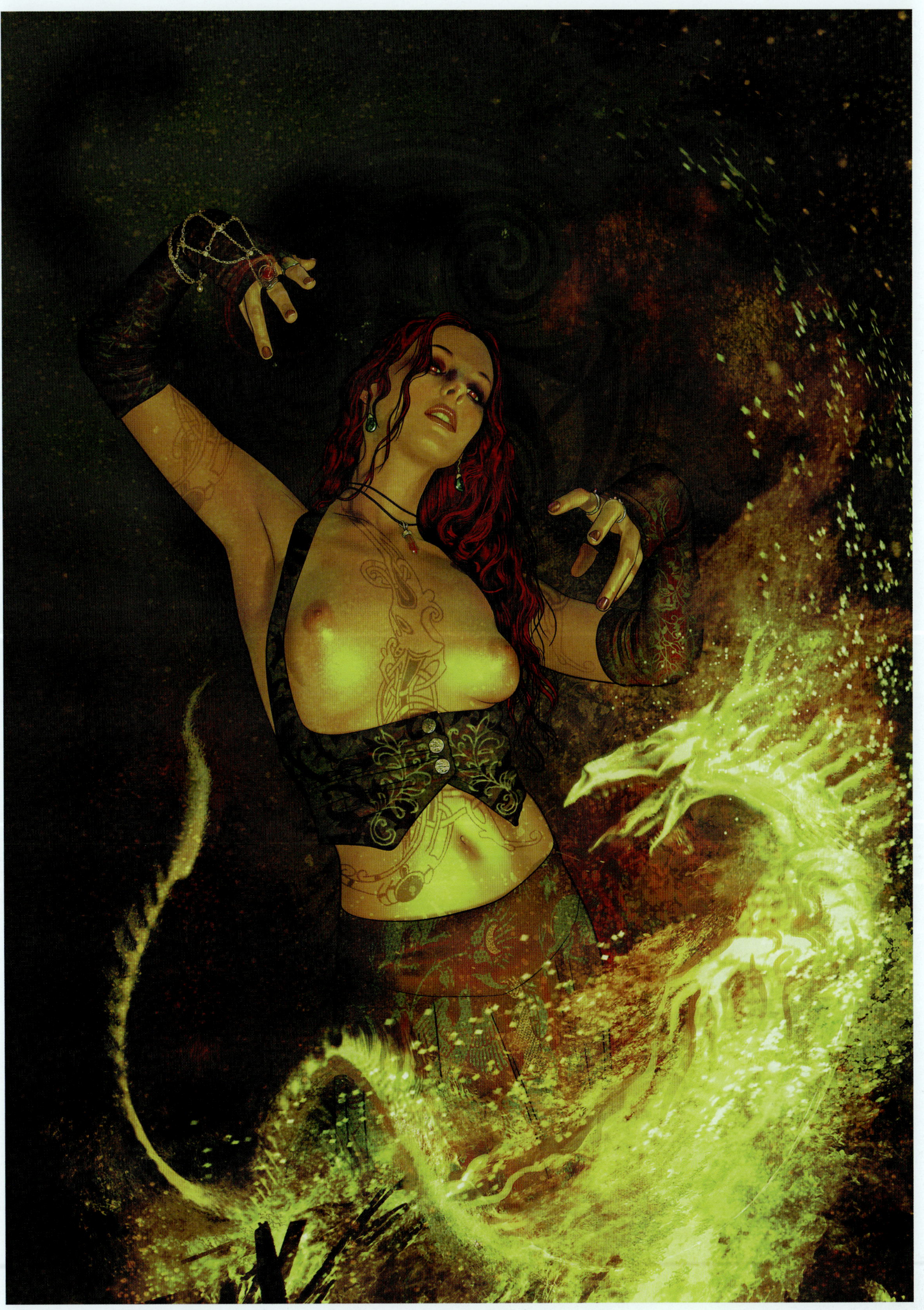

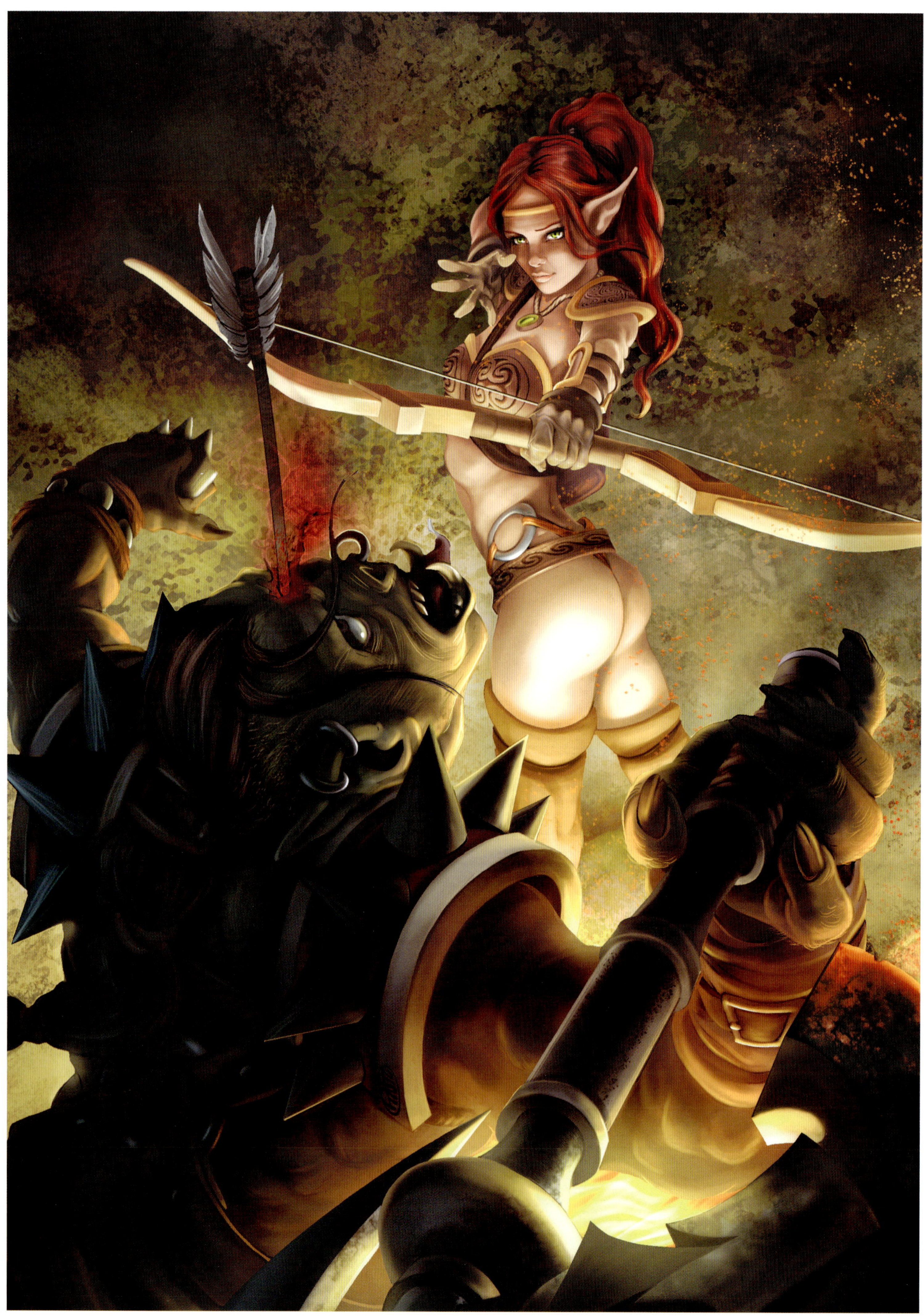

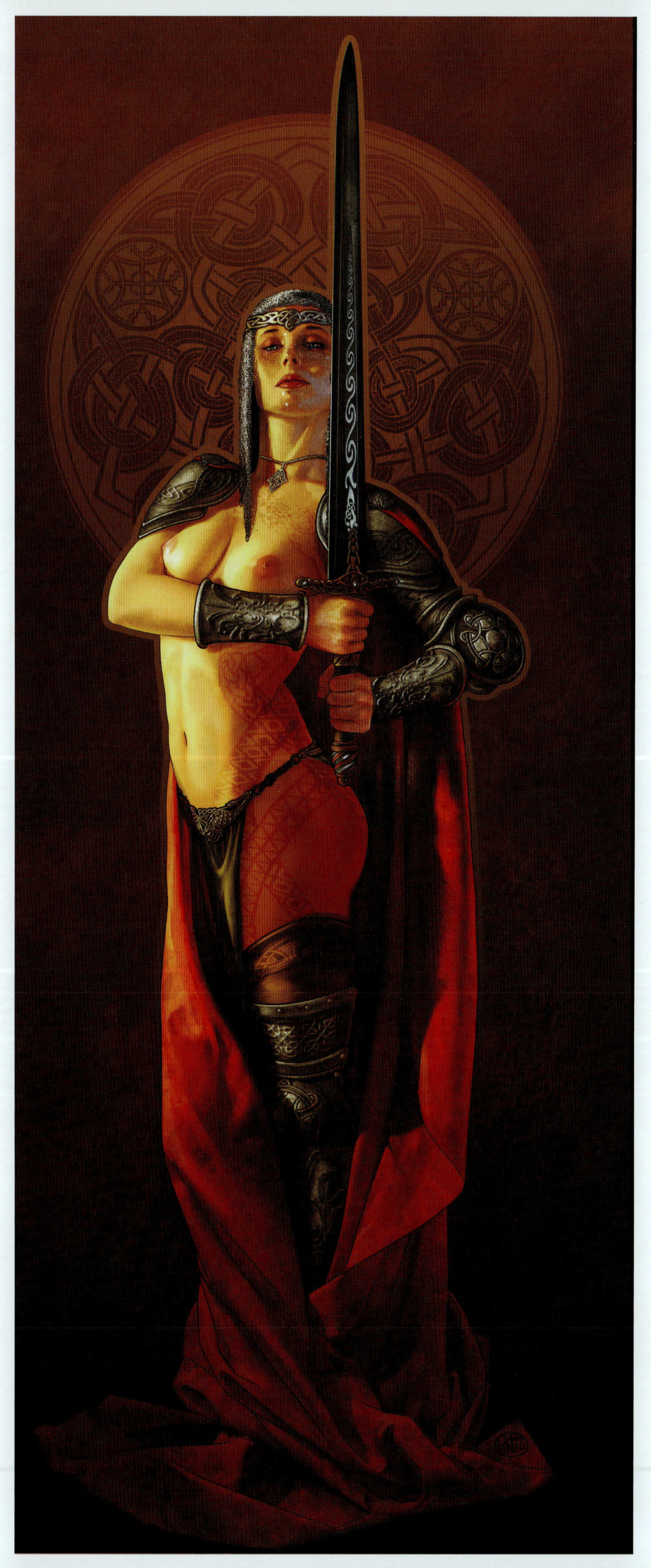

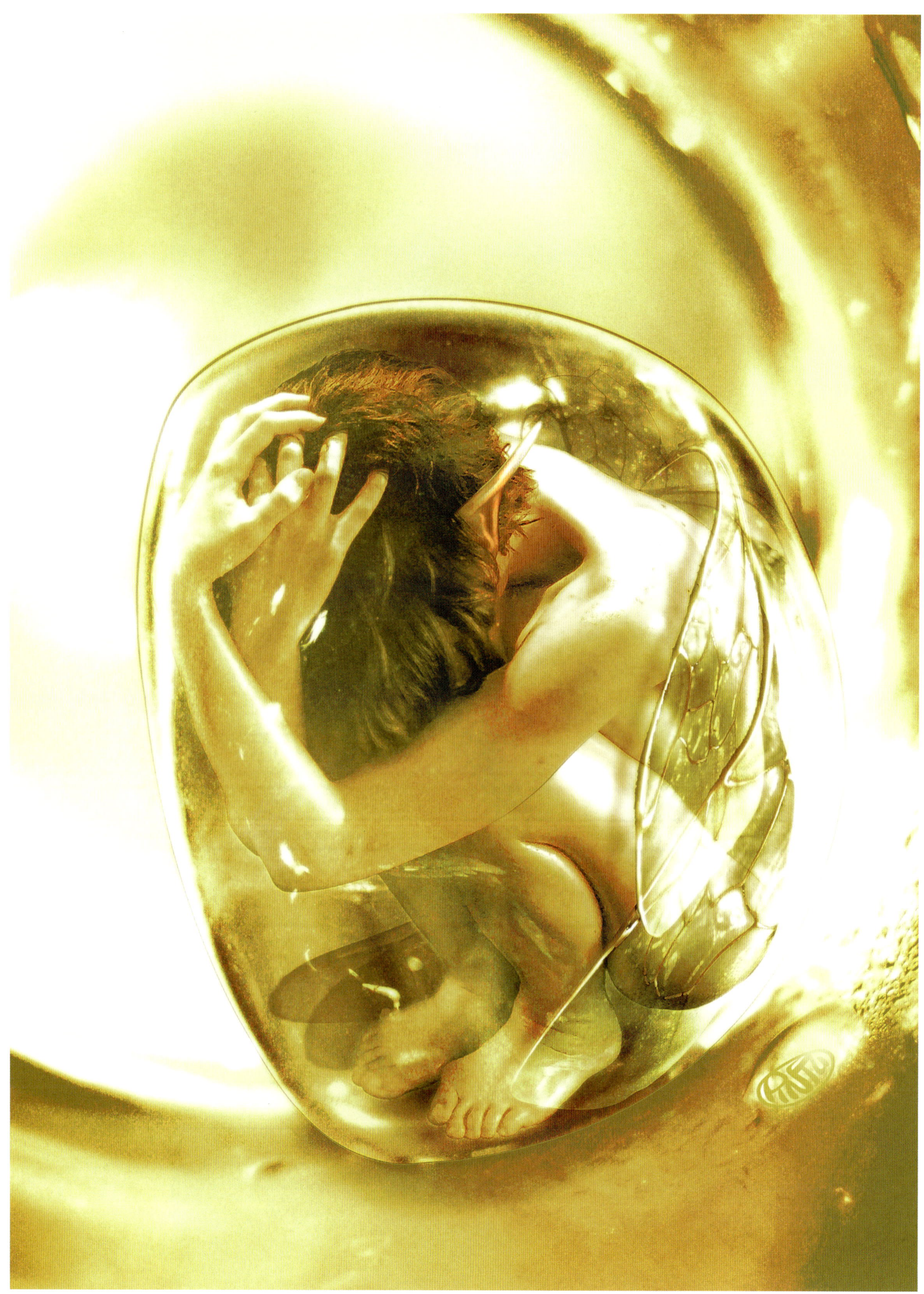

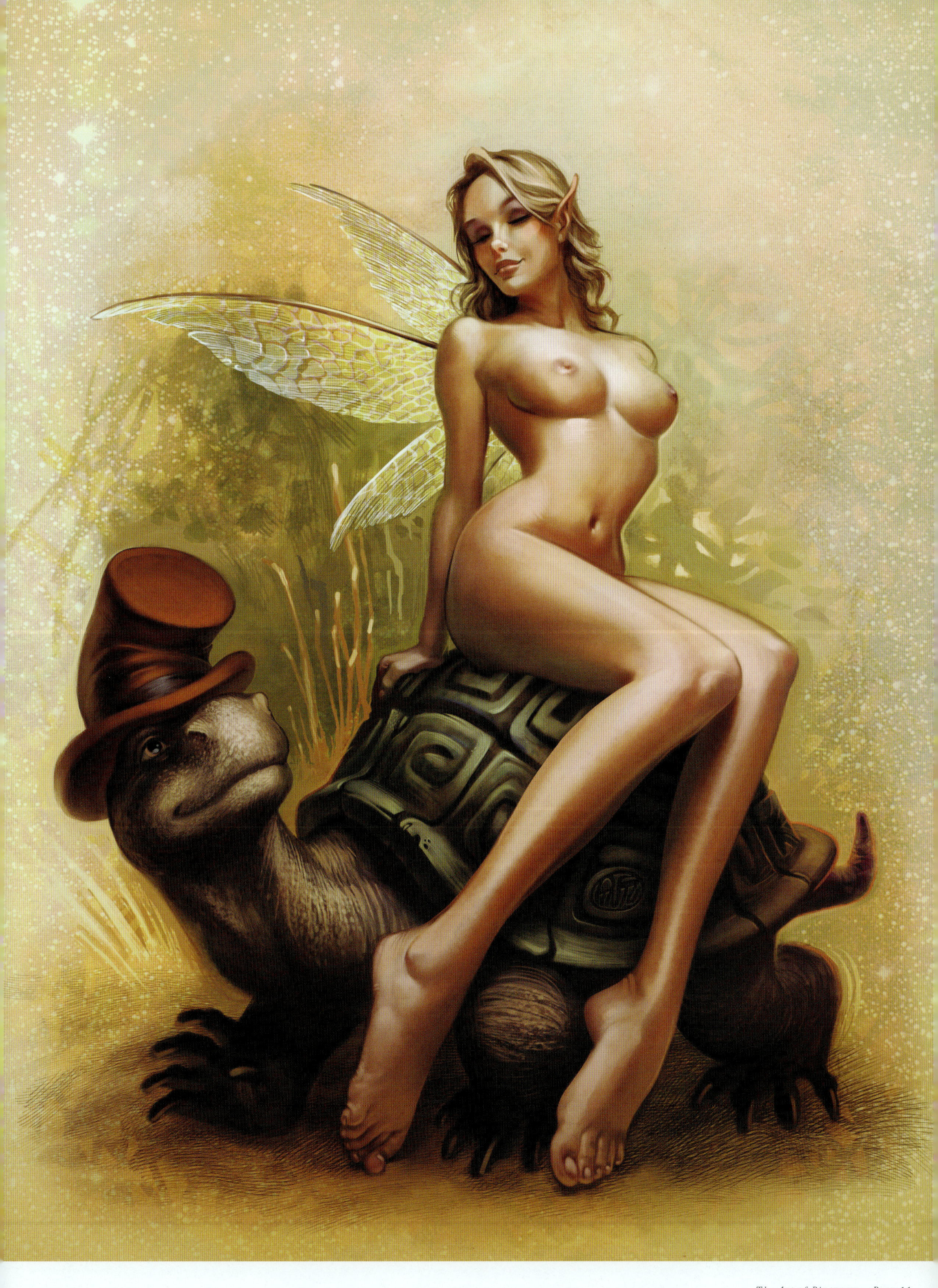

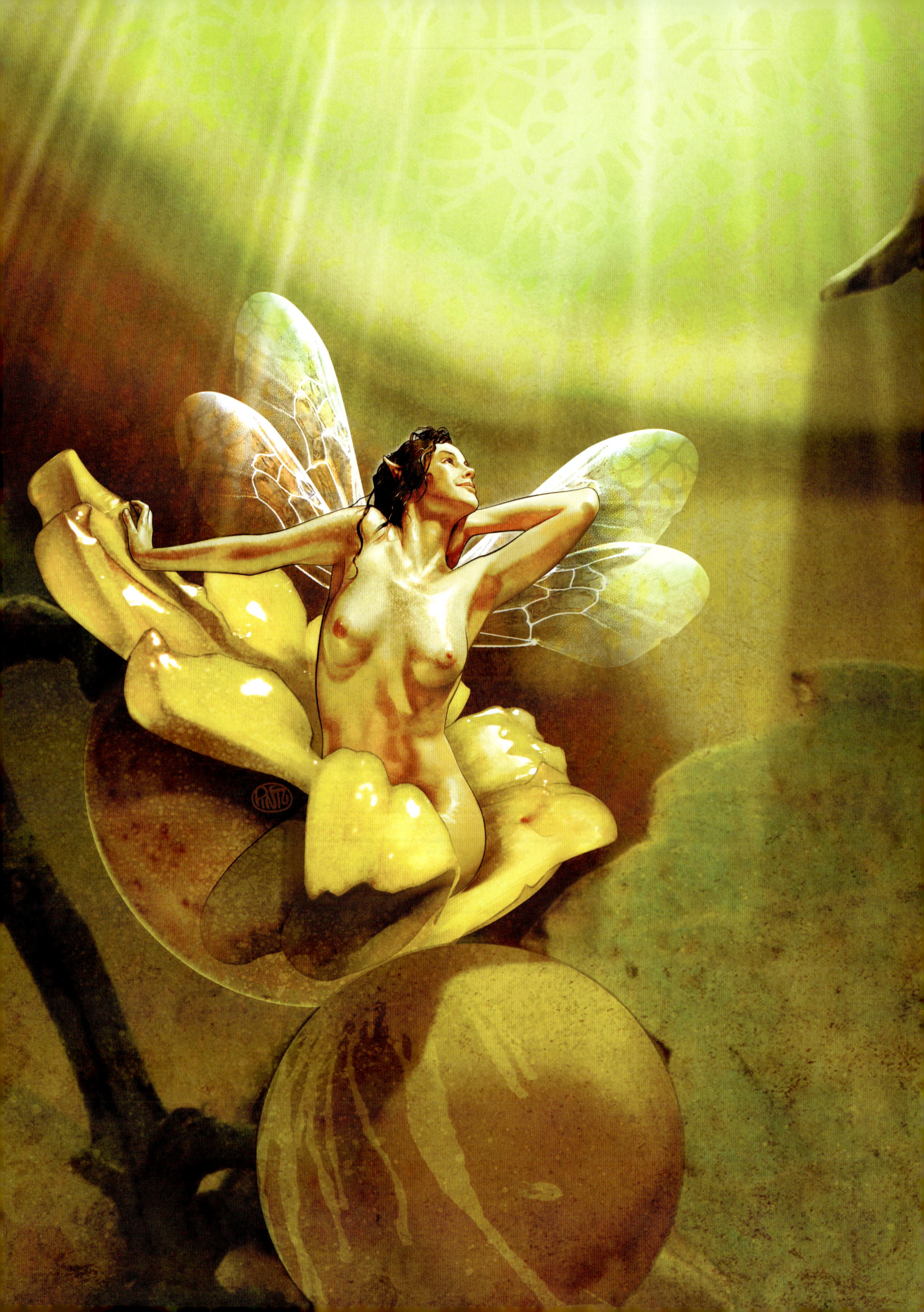

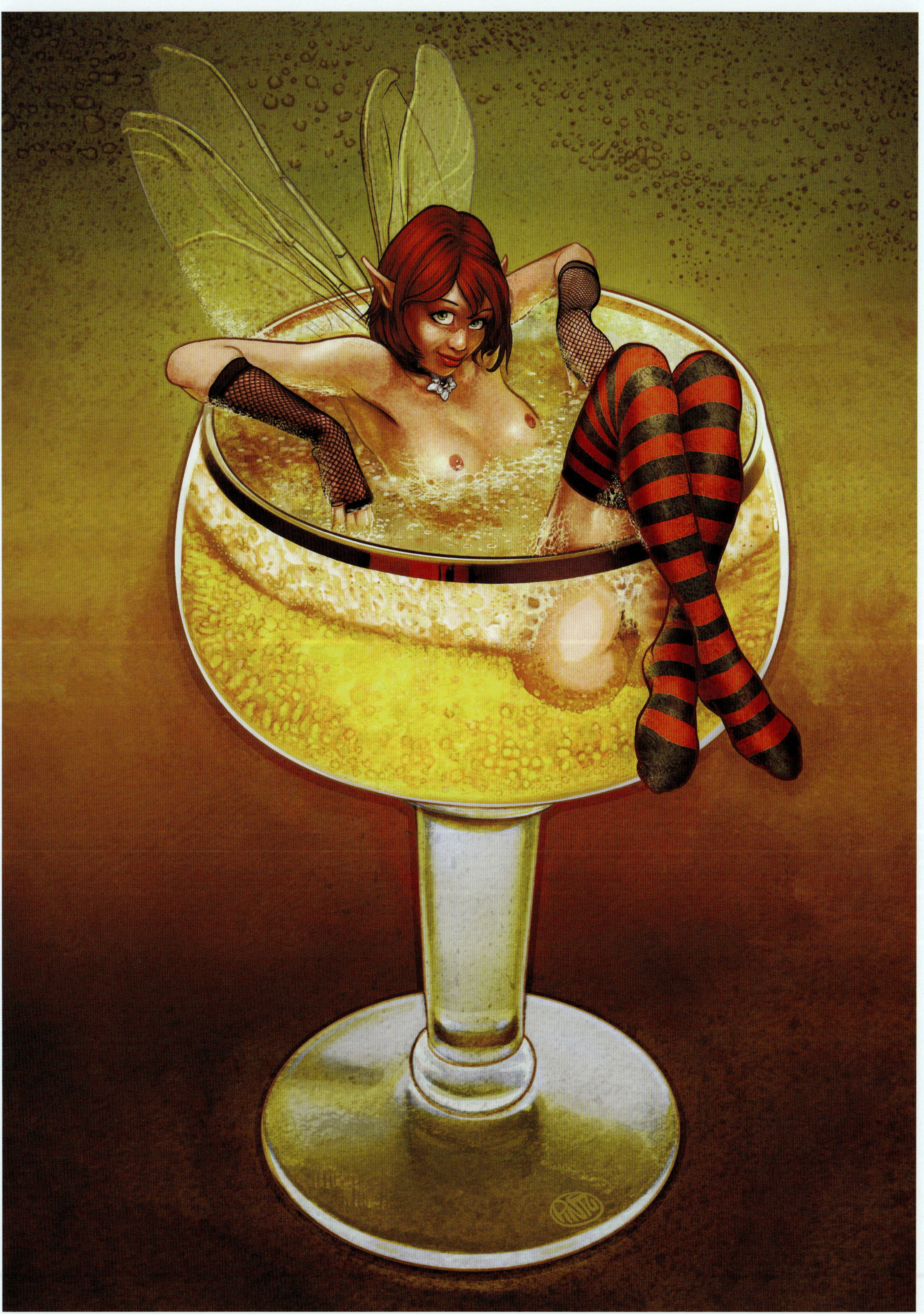

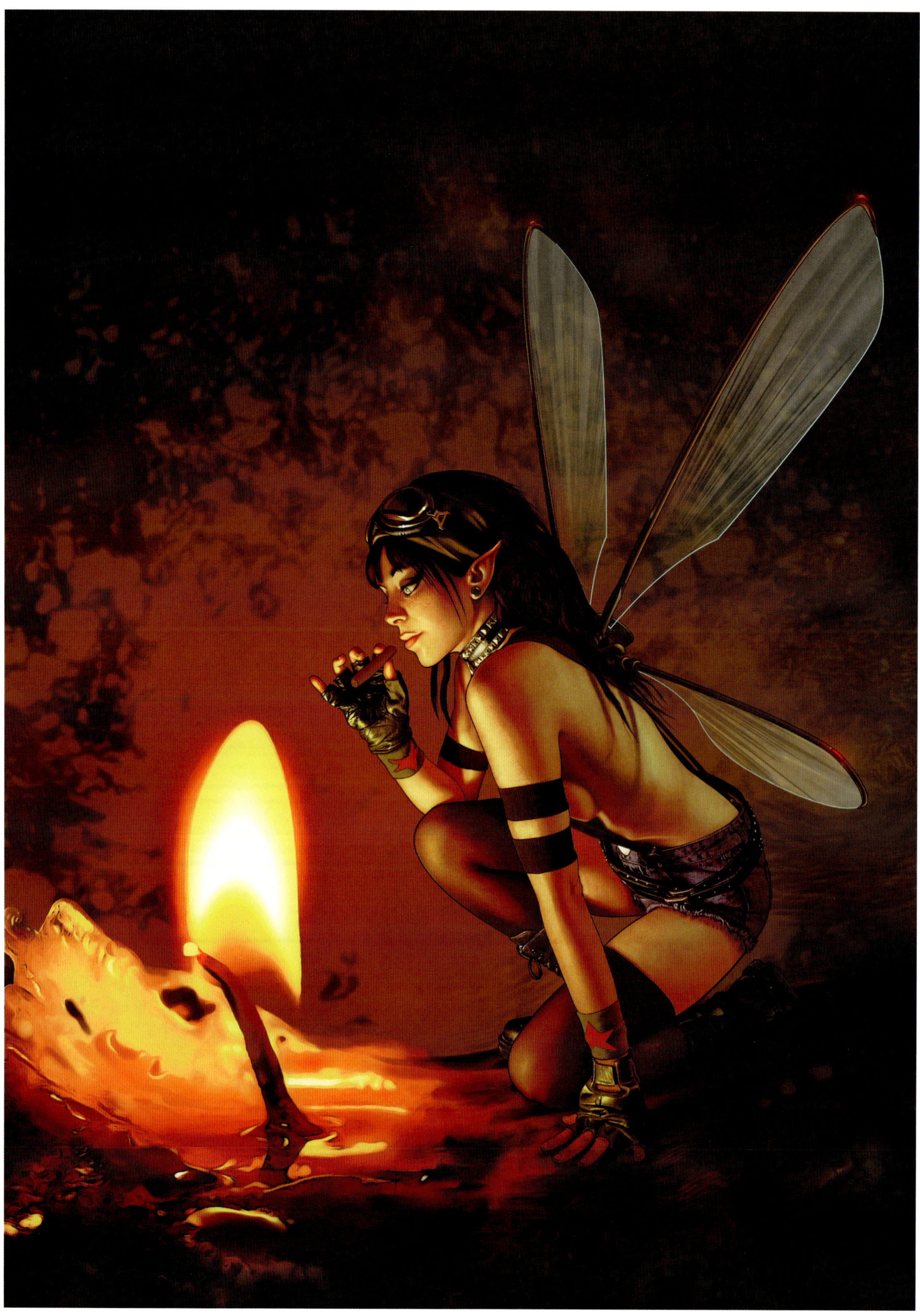

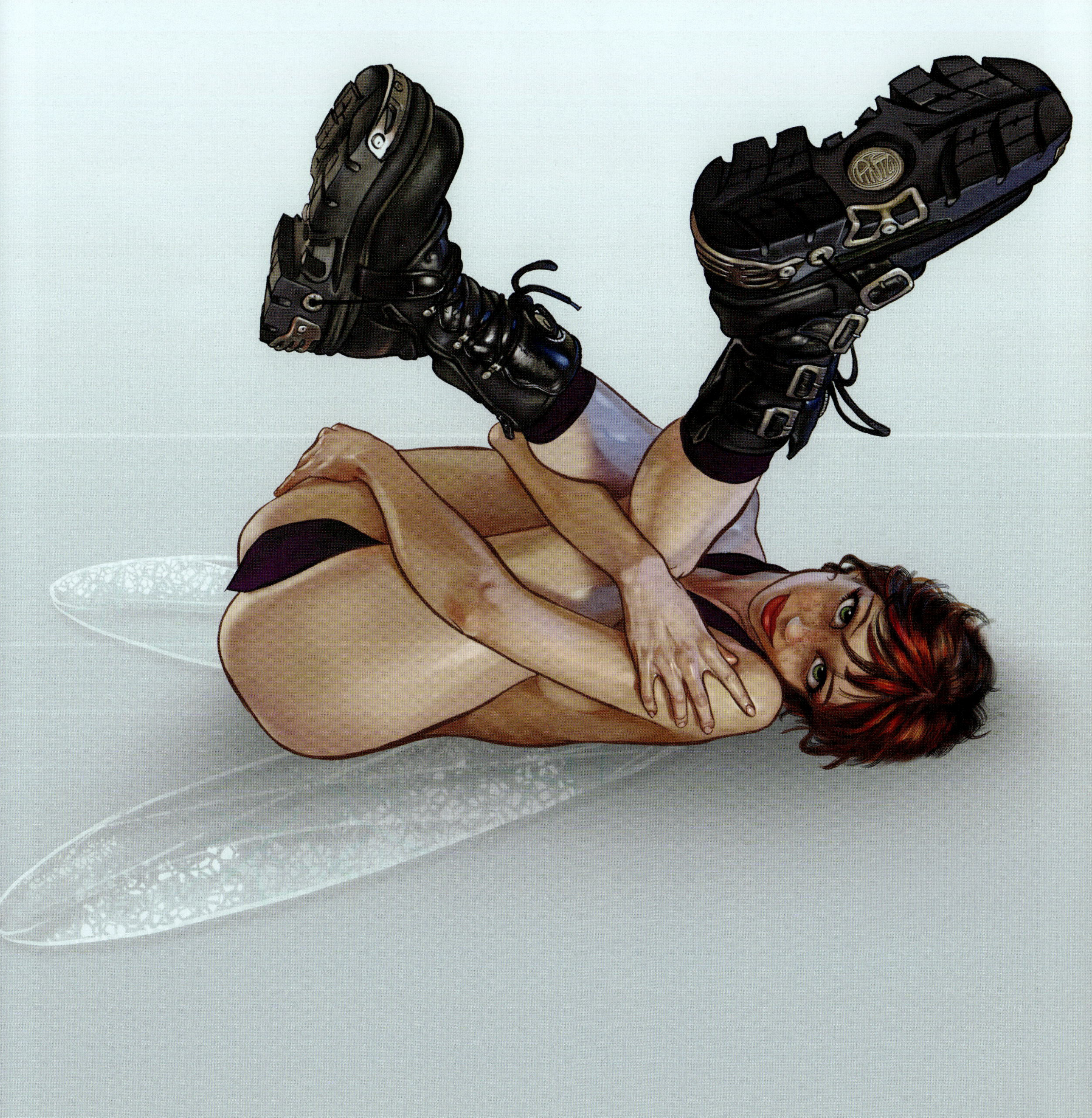

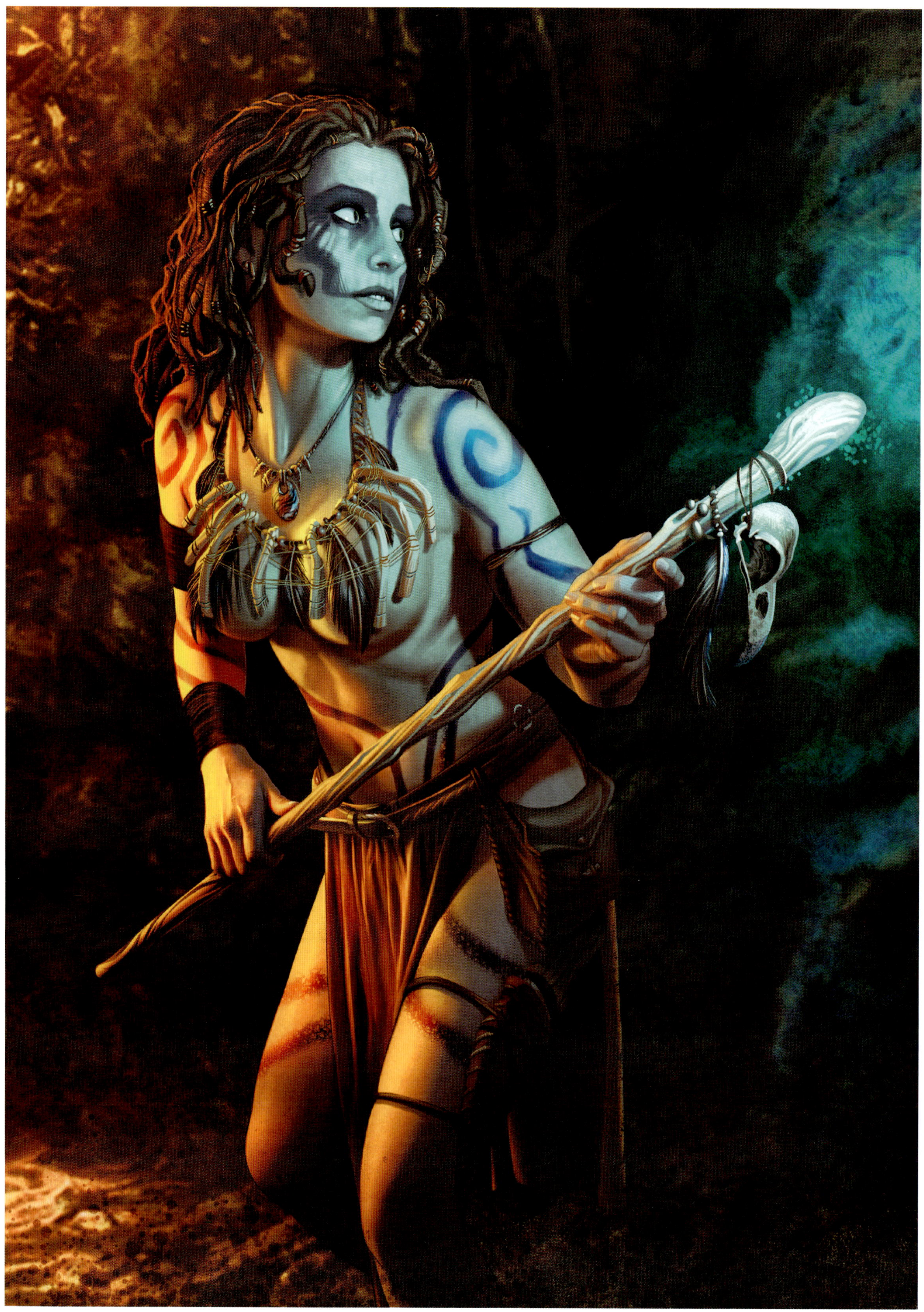

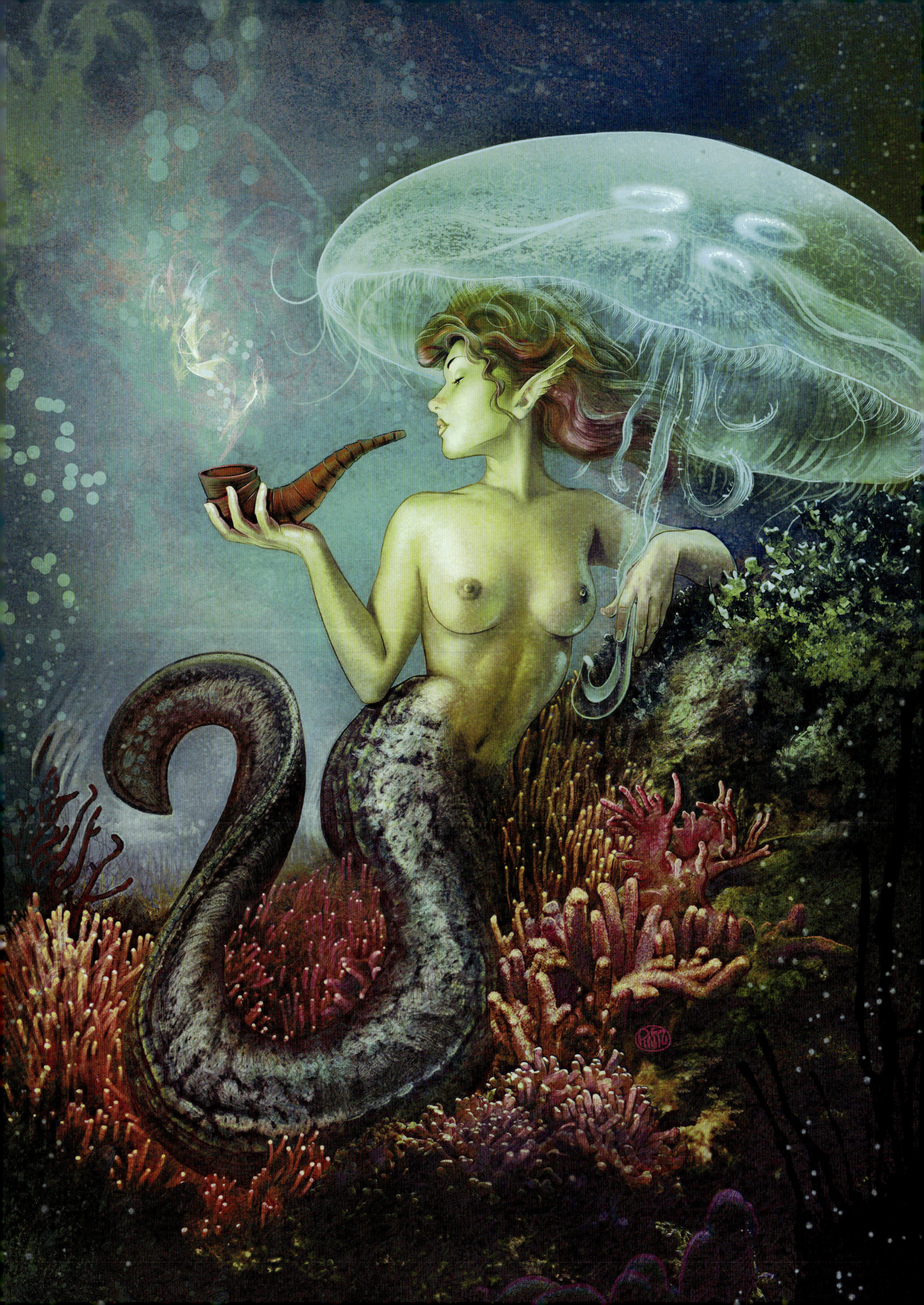

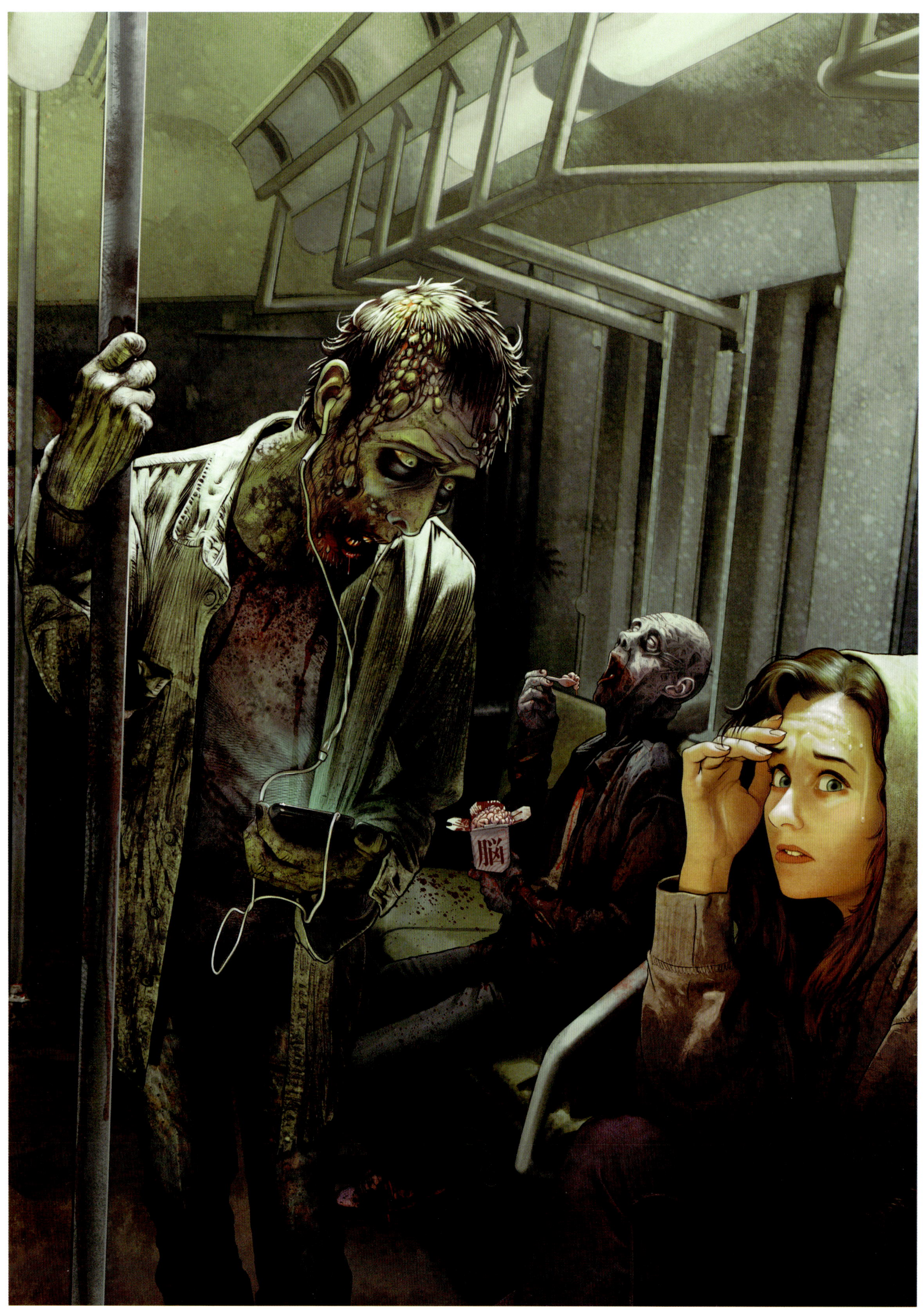
脑

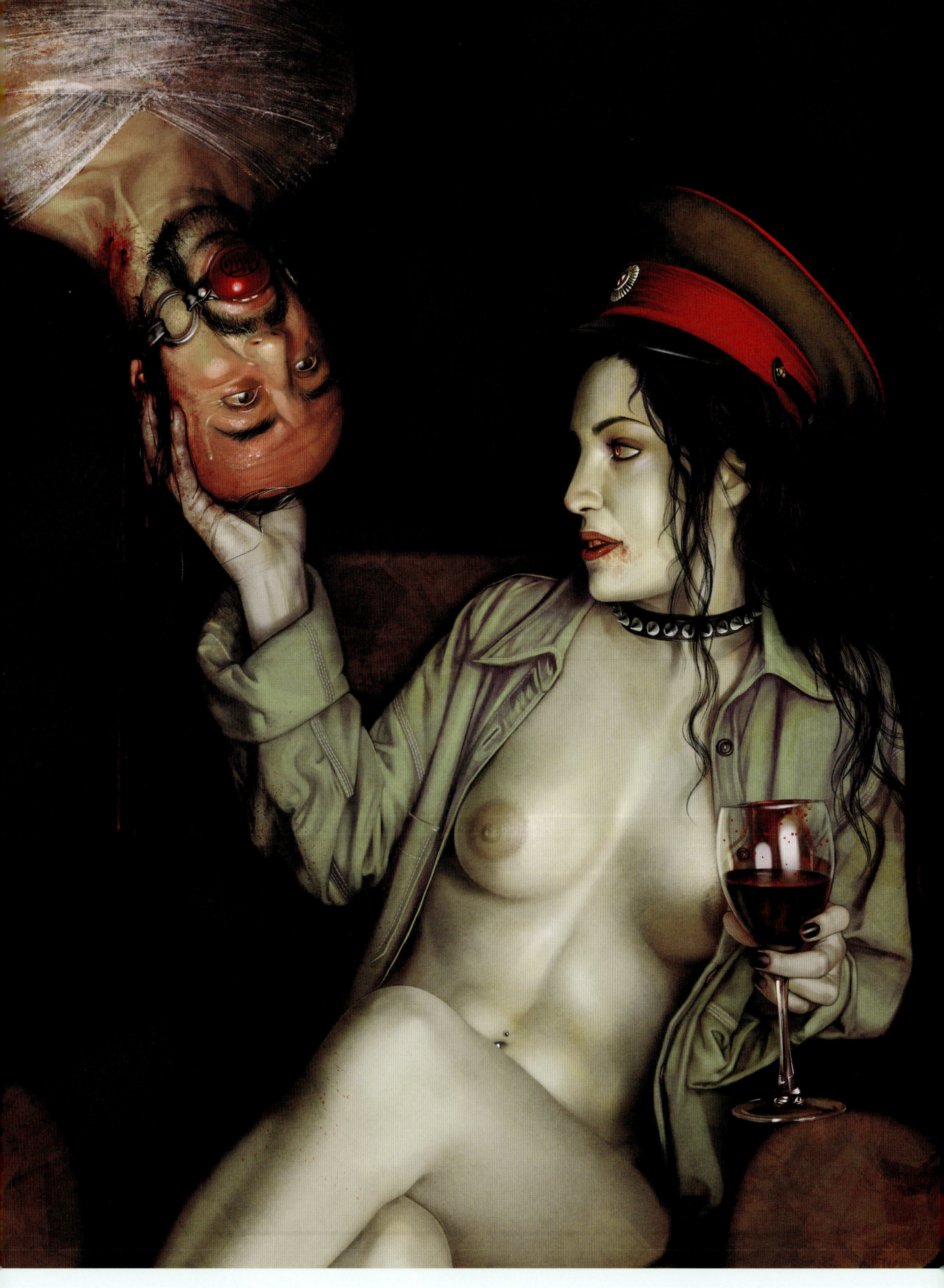

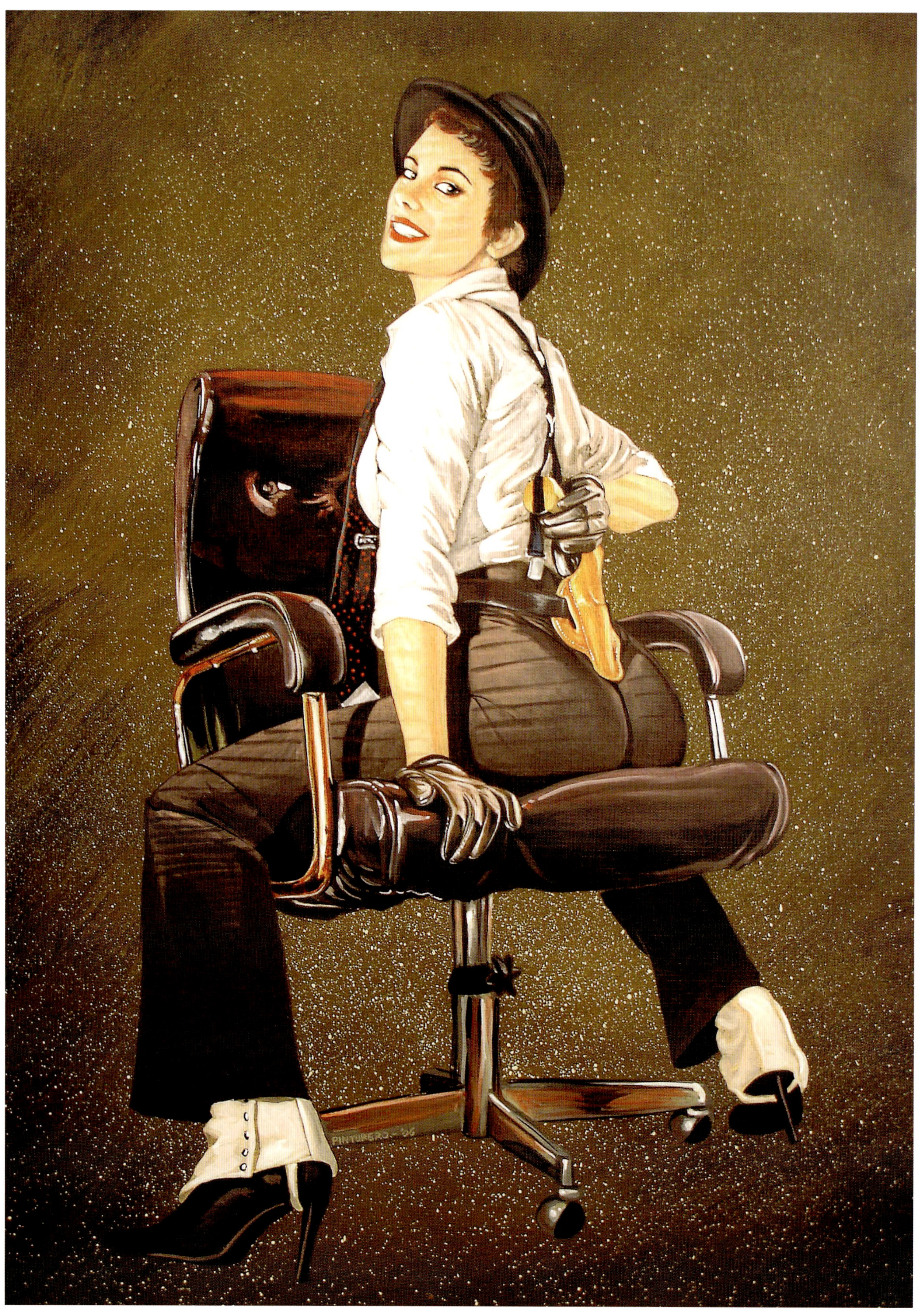

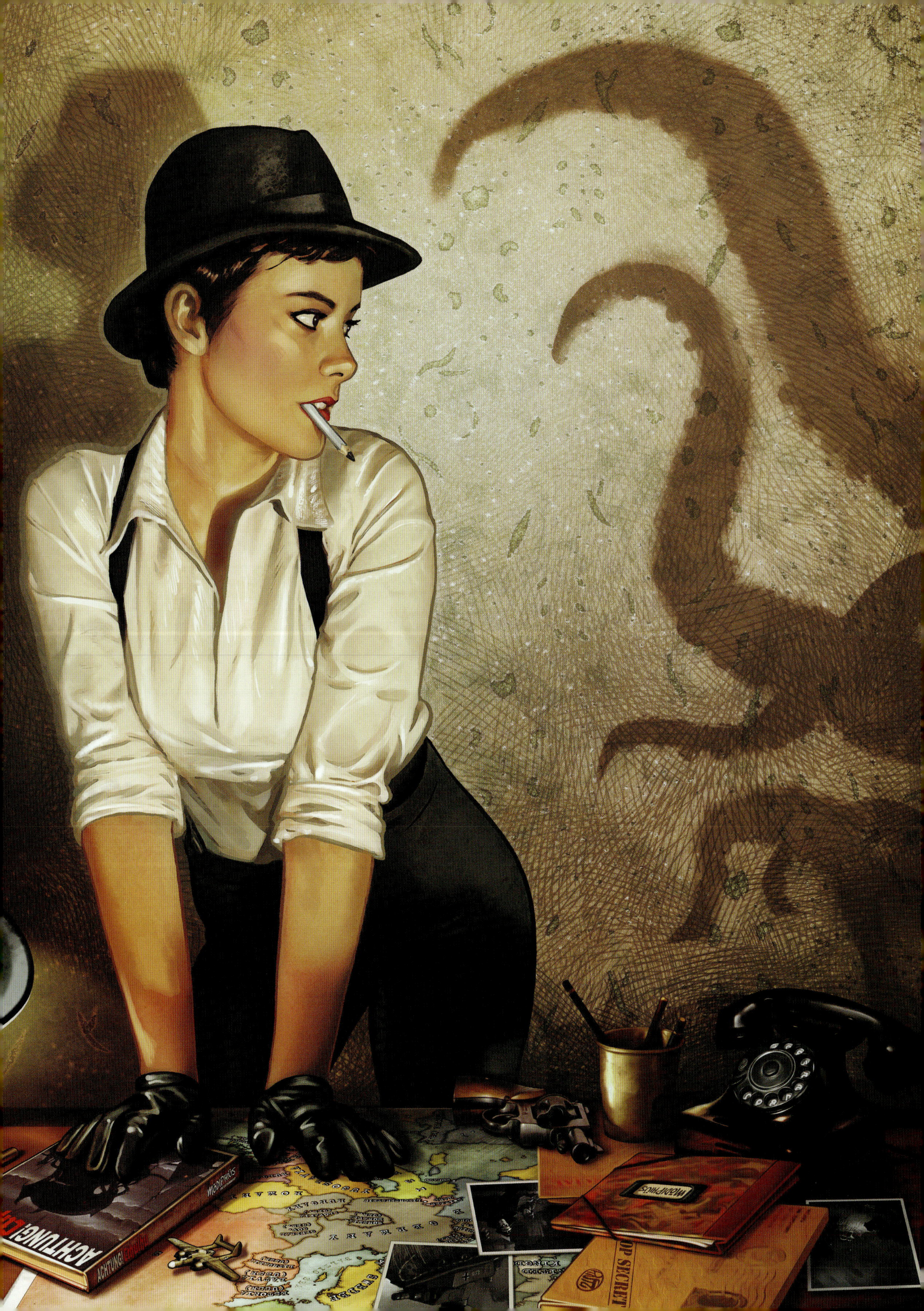

ACHTUNG!
MODIPHIUS
ACHTUNG!
YUGOSLAVIA
HUNGARY
GERMANY
SWEDEN
MODIPHIUS
OP SECRET

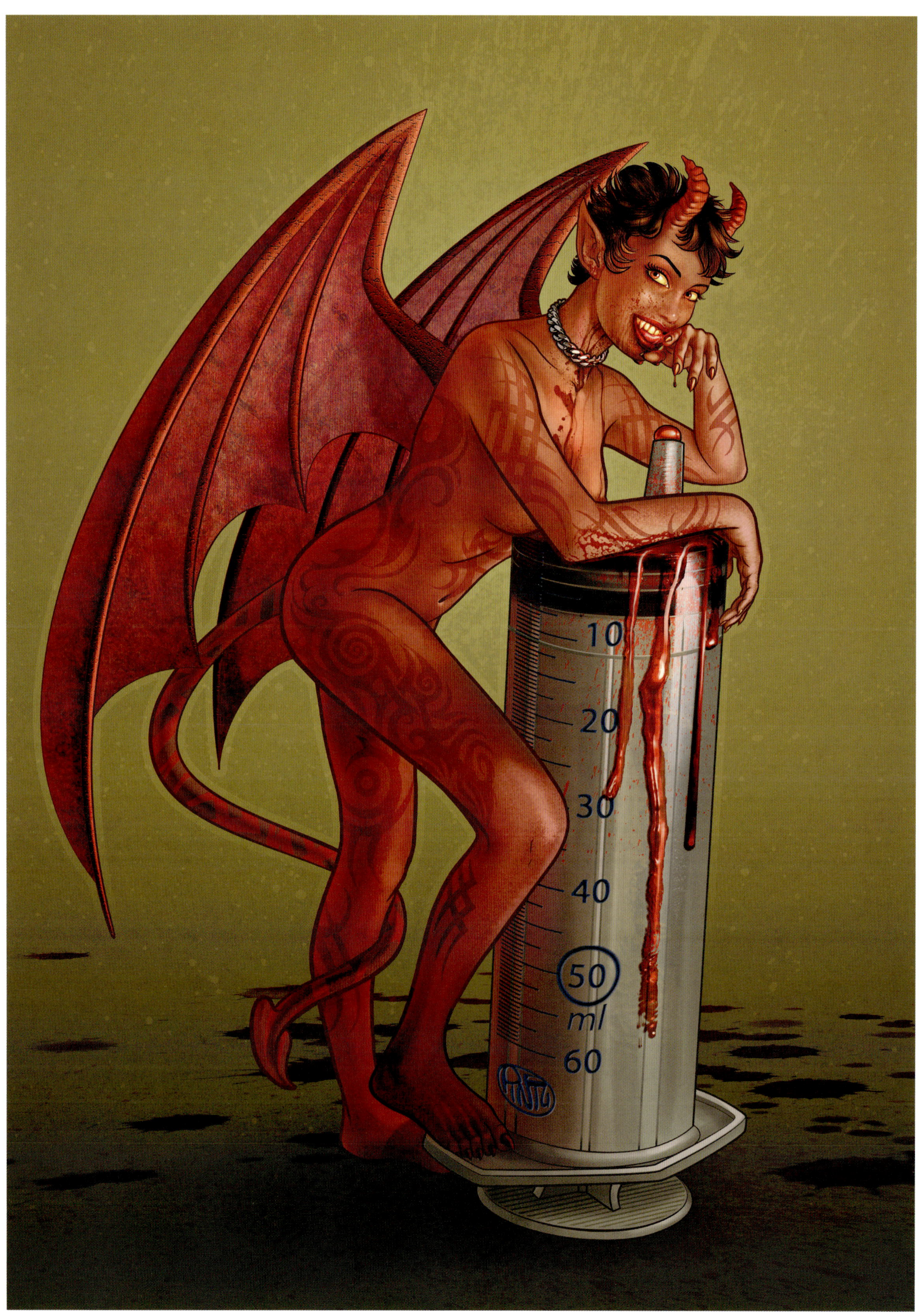
10
20
30
40
50
ml
60

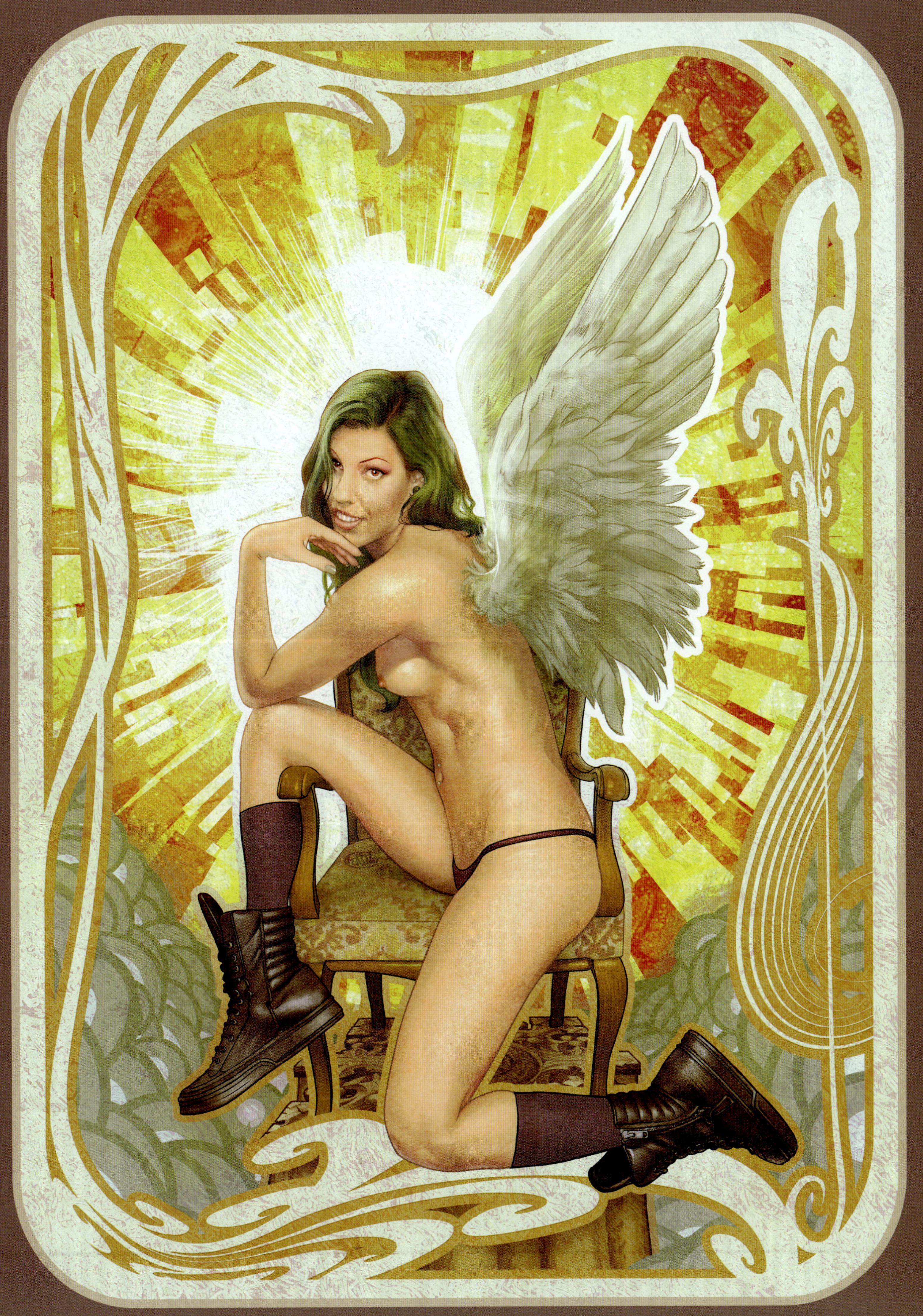

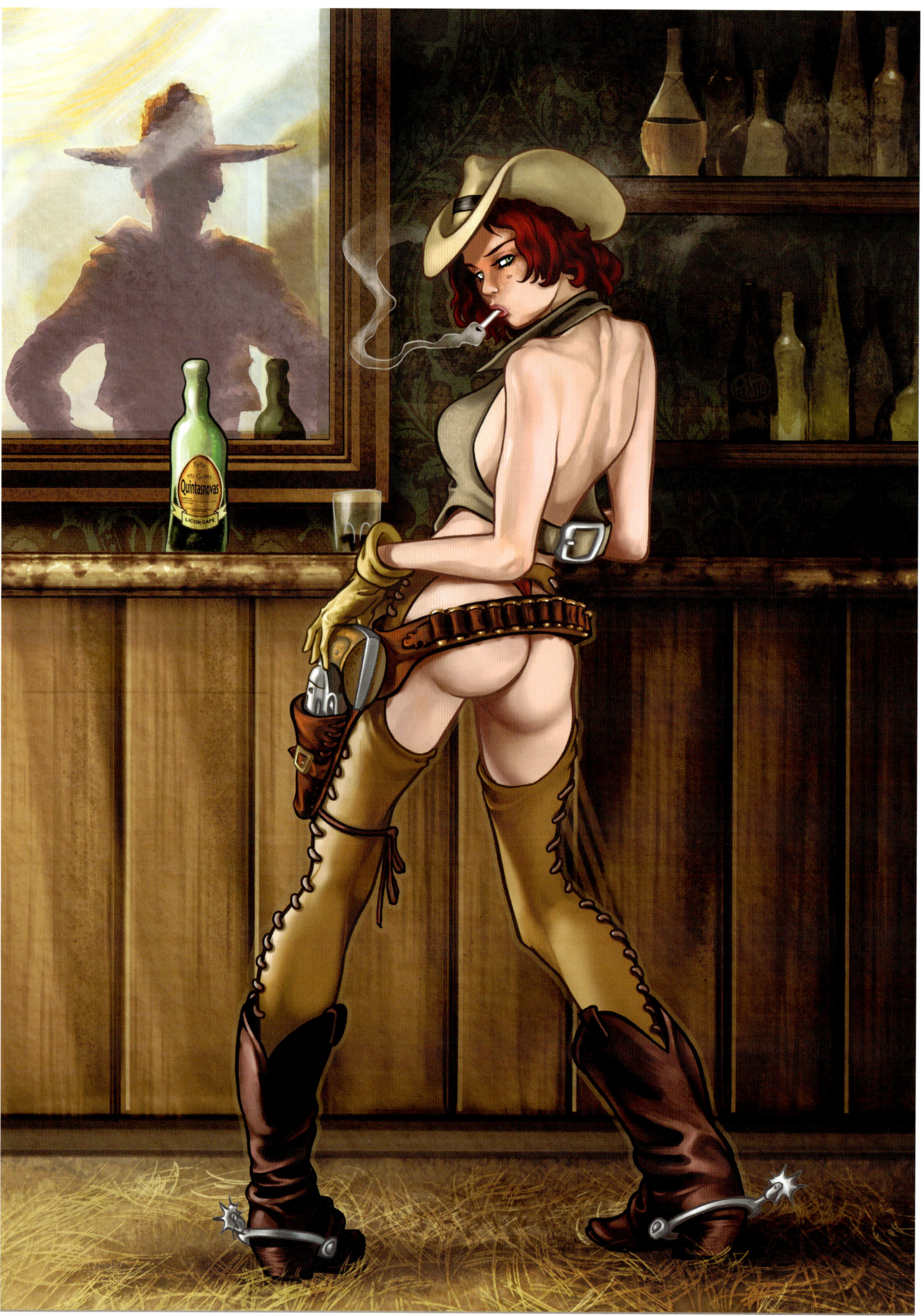
Quintasnovas
LICOR CAFÉ

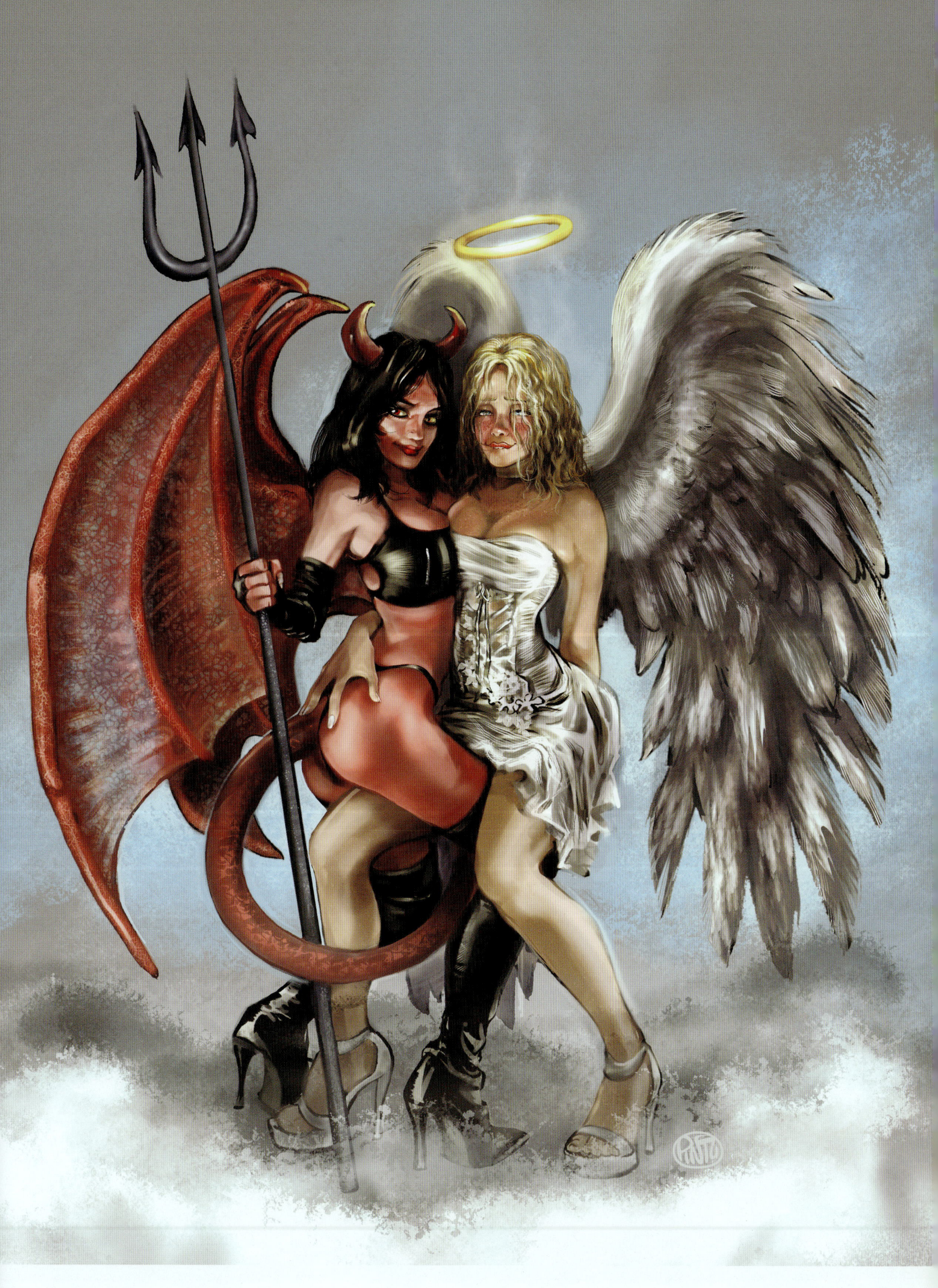

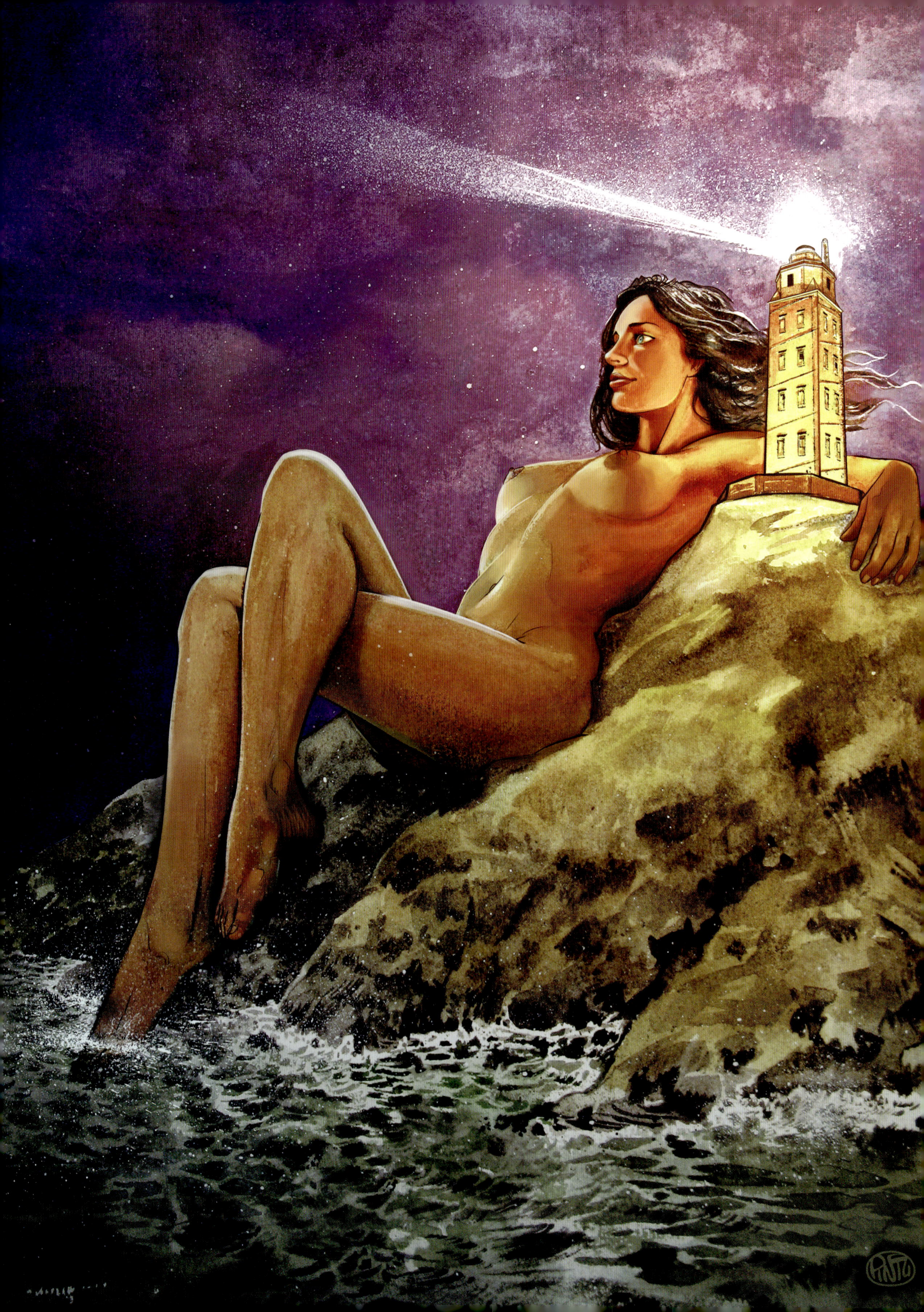

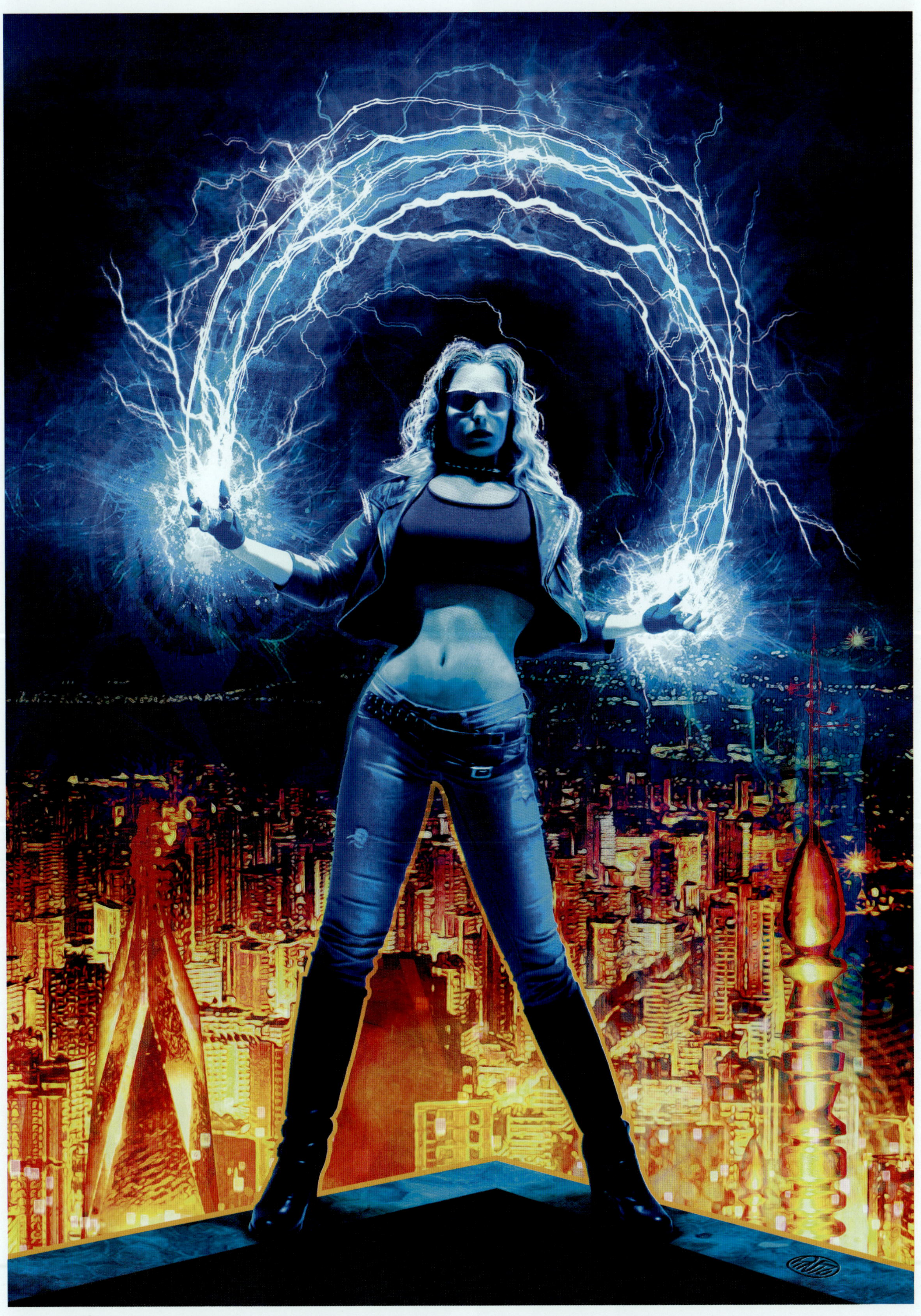

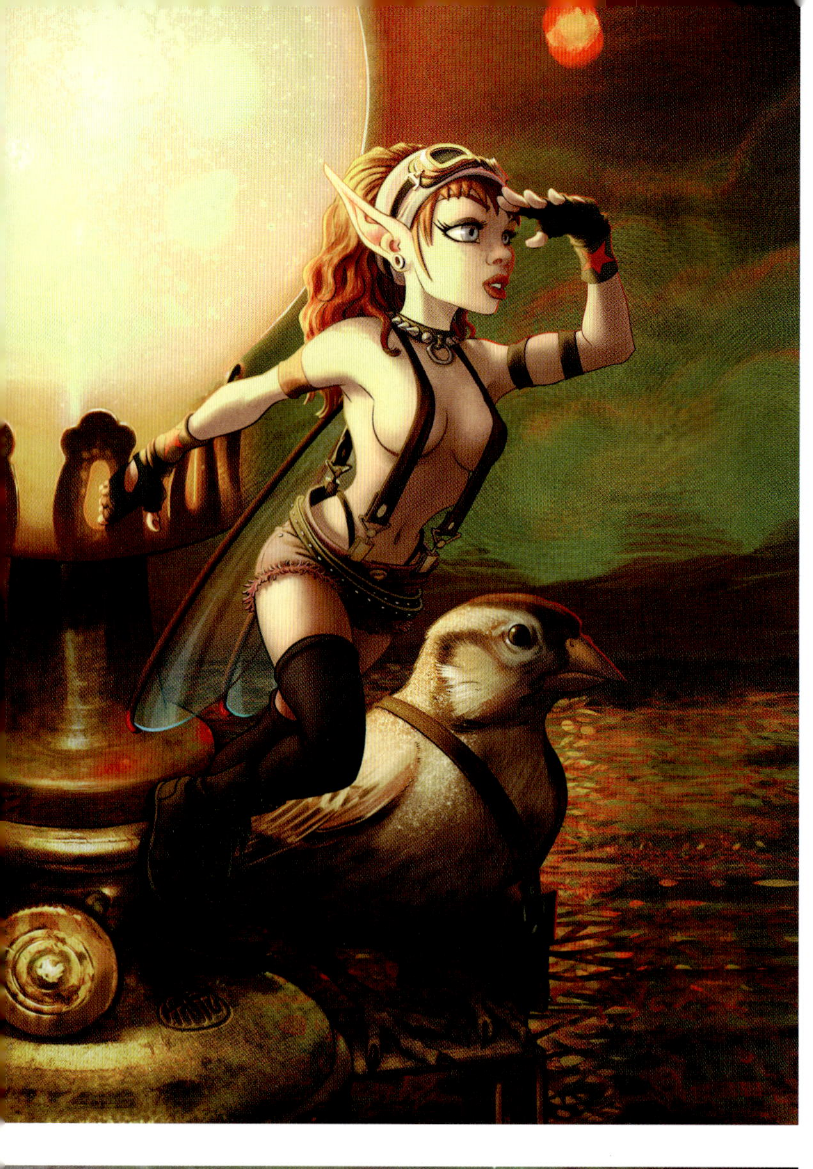

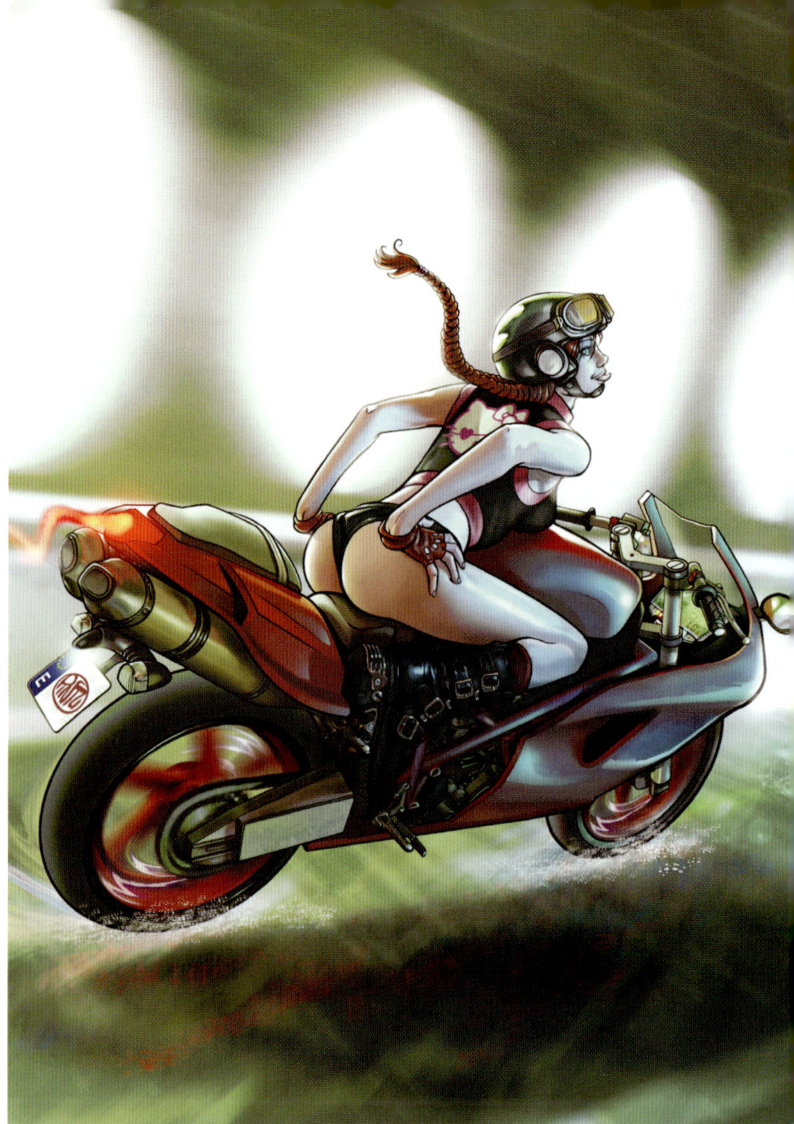

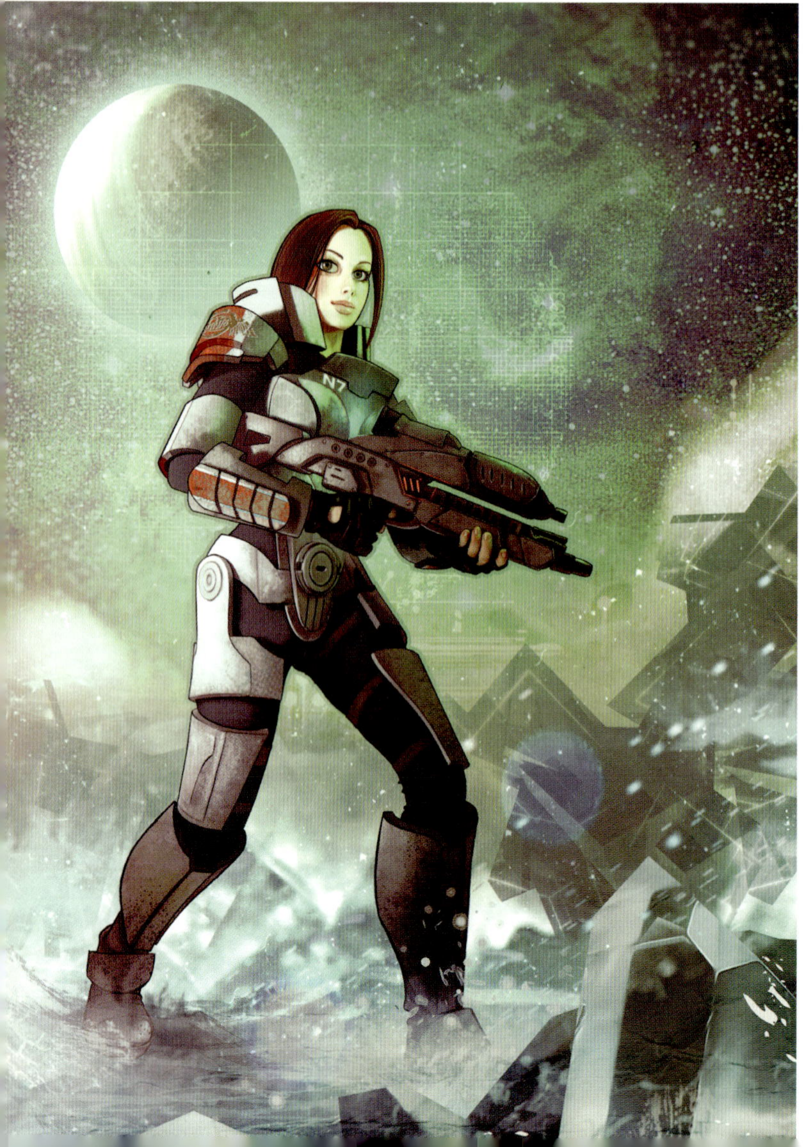

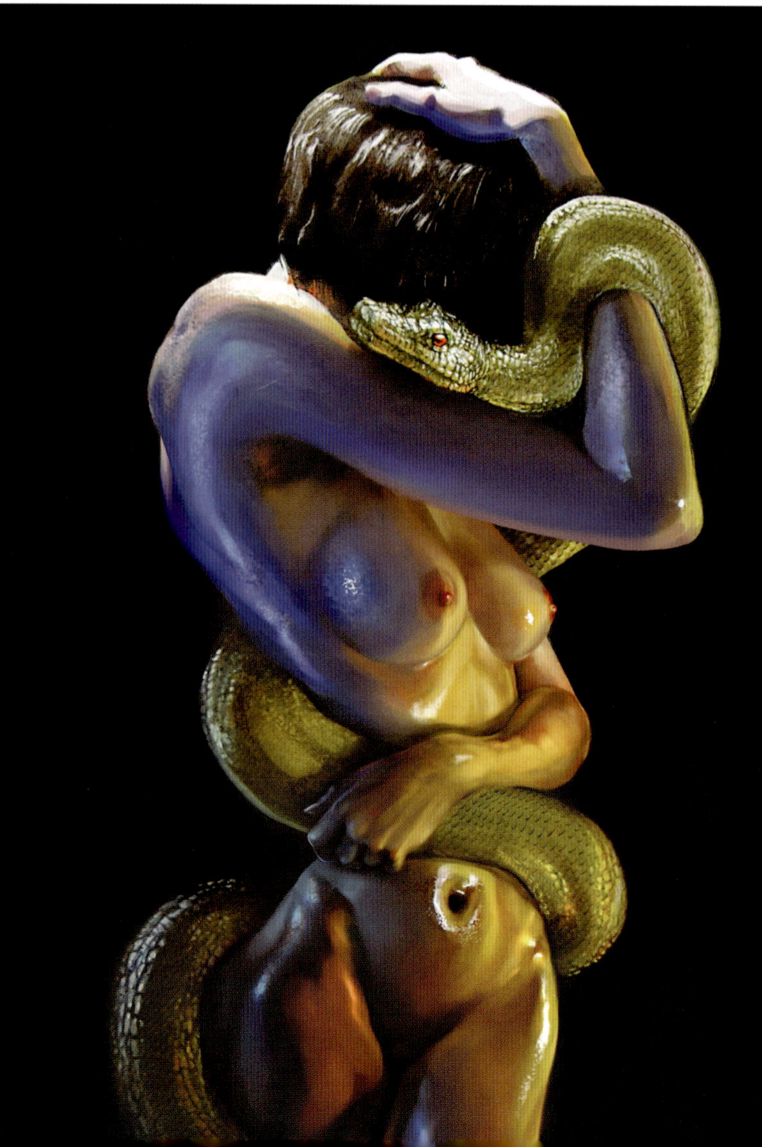

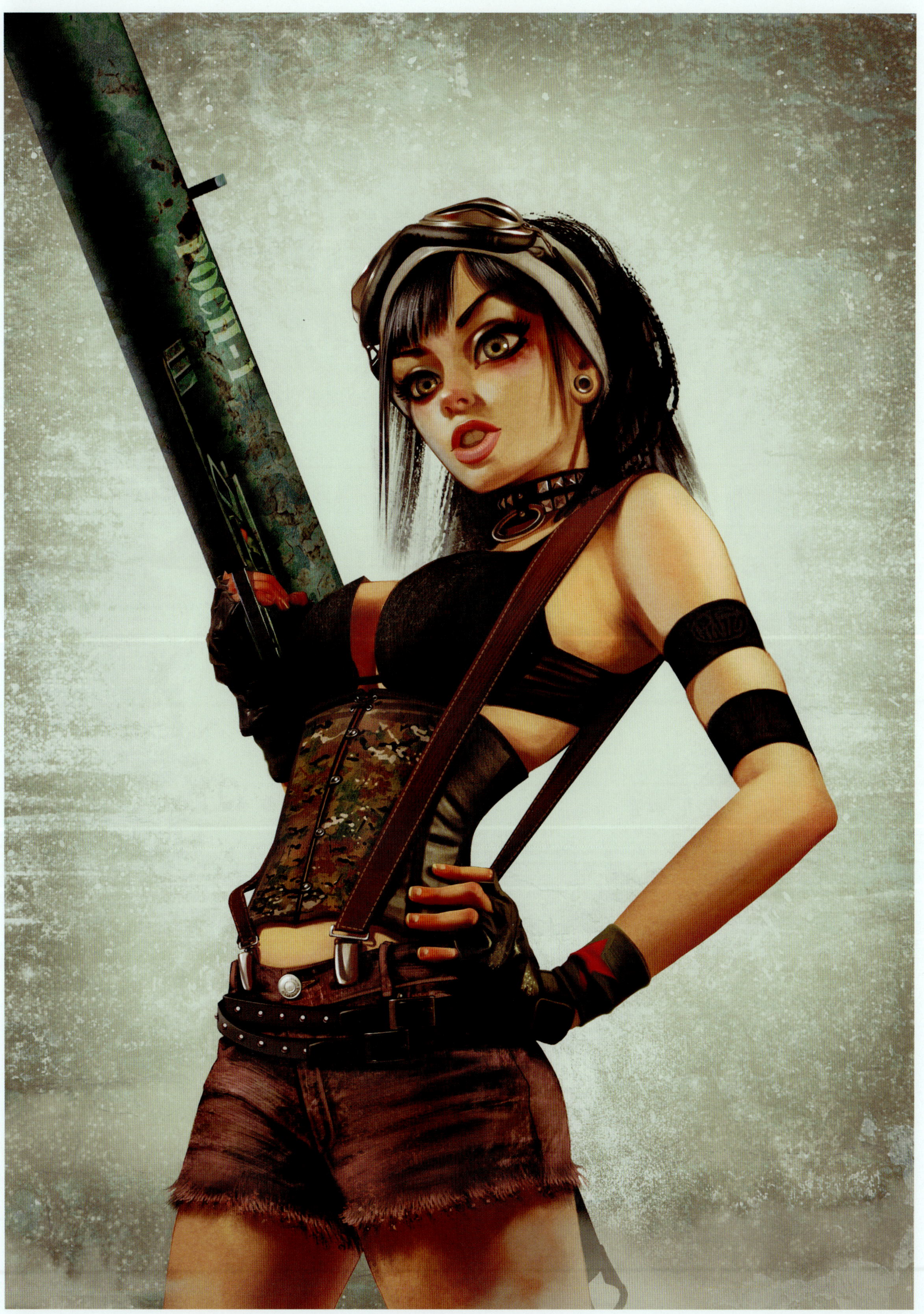

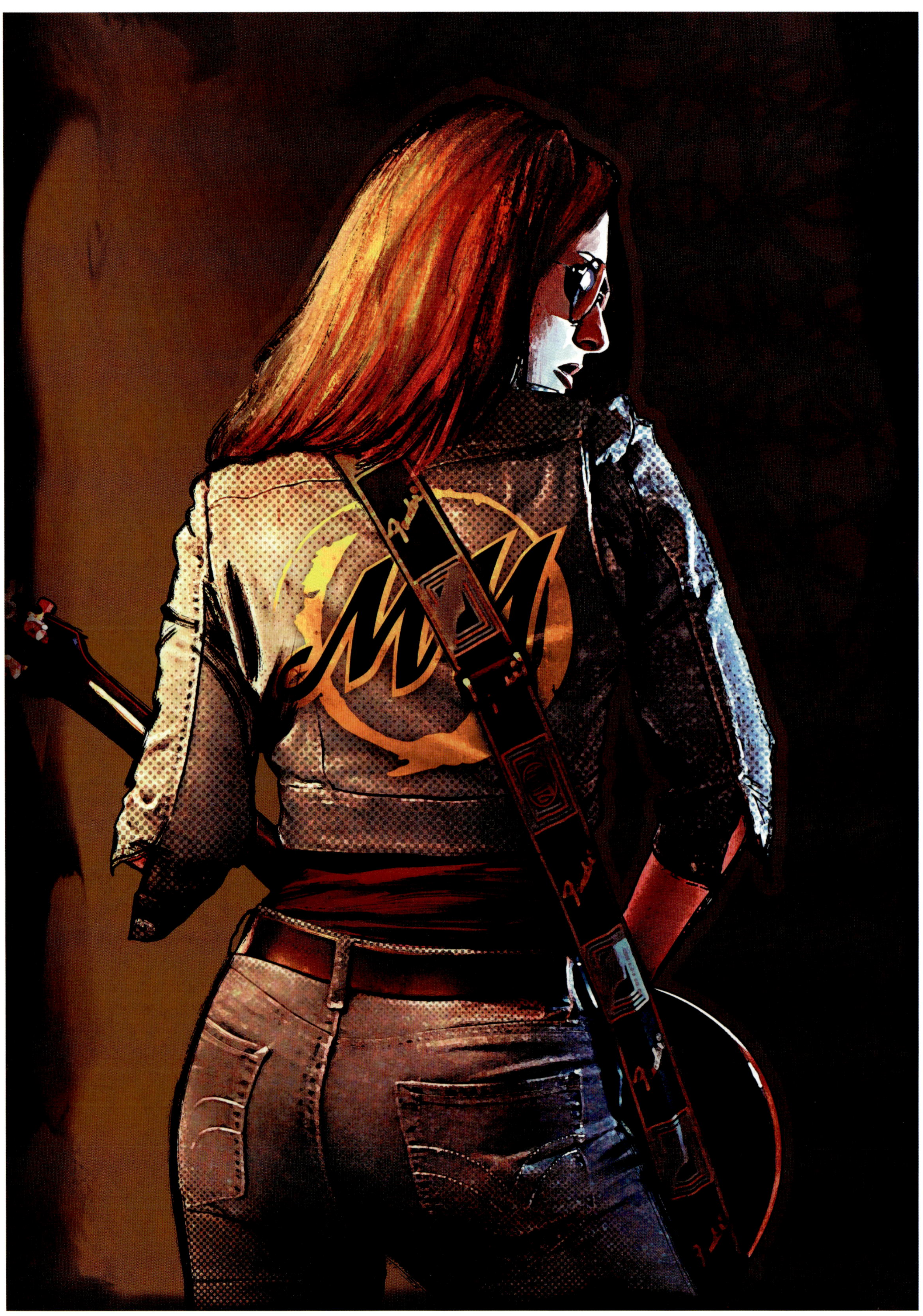

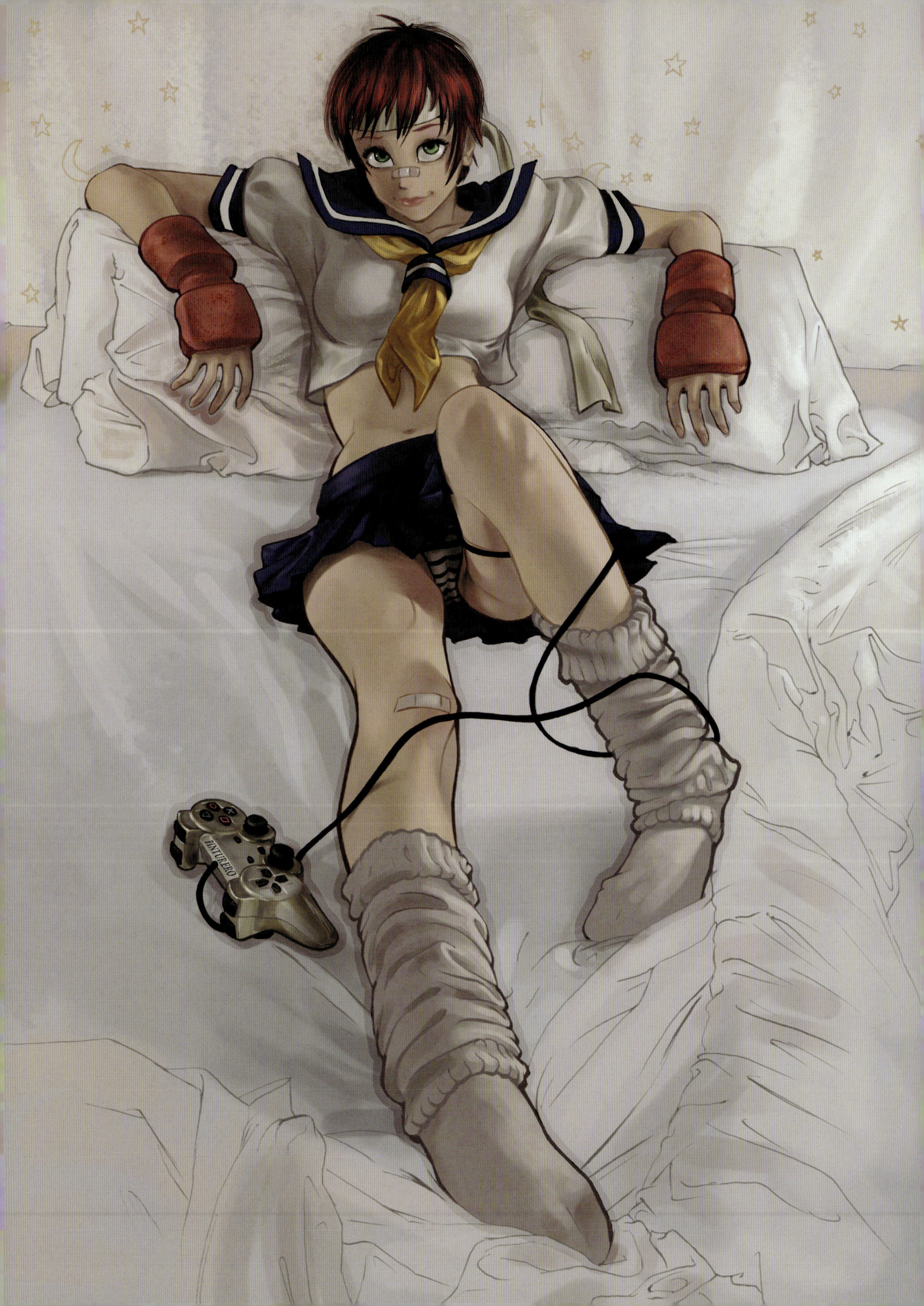
PINTURERO

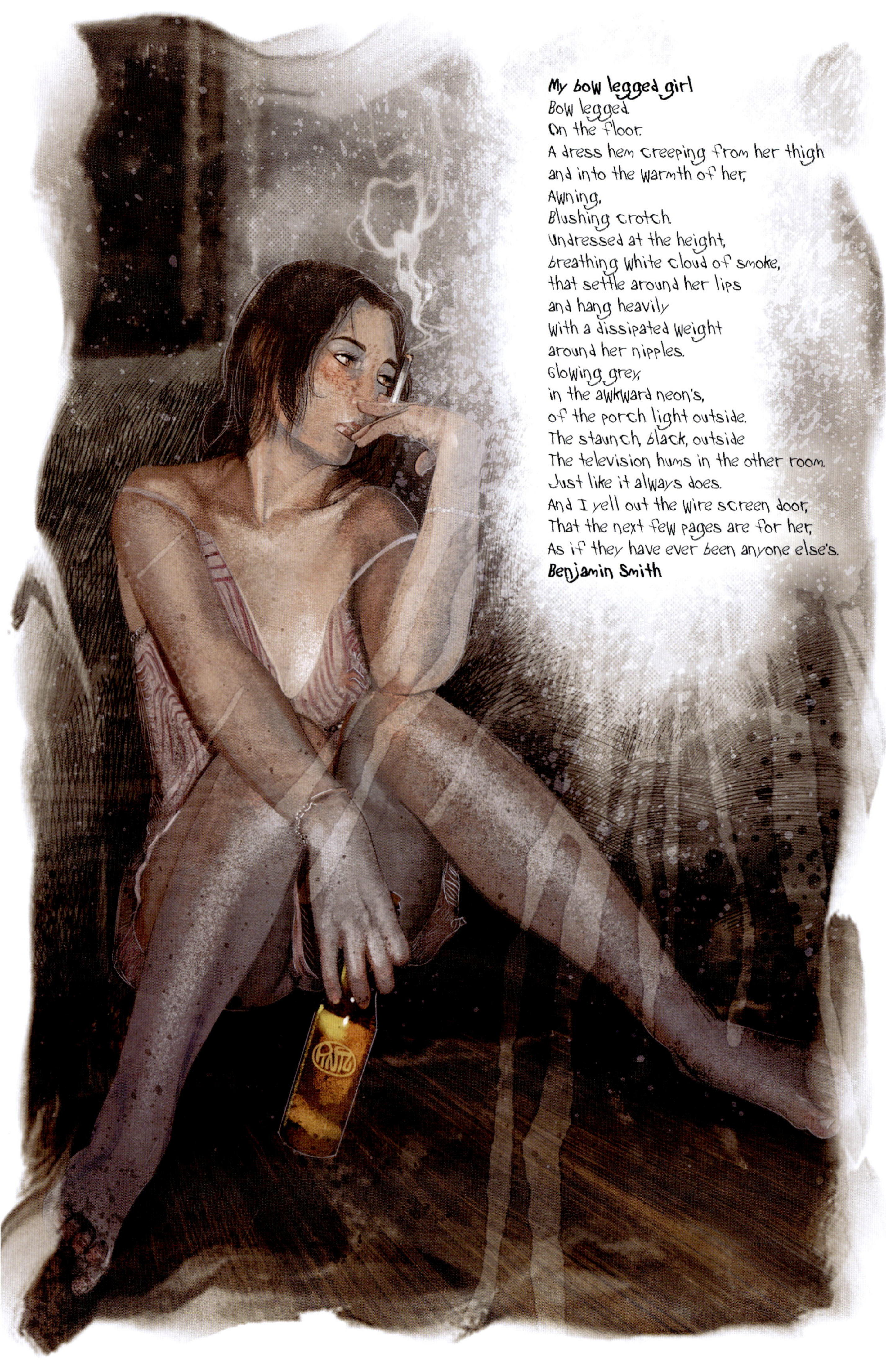
My bow legged girl
Bow legged
On the floor.
A dress hem creeping from her thigh
and into the warmth of her,
Awning,
Blushing crotch
Undressed at the height,
breathing white cloud of smoke,
that settle around her lips
and hang heavily
With a dissipated weight
around her nipples.
Glowing grey,
in the awkward neon's,
of the porch light outside.
The staunch, black, outside
The television hums in the other room.
Just like it always does.
And I yell out the wire screen door,
That the next few pages are for her,
As if they have ever been anyone else's.
Benjamin Smith

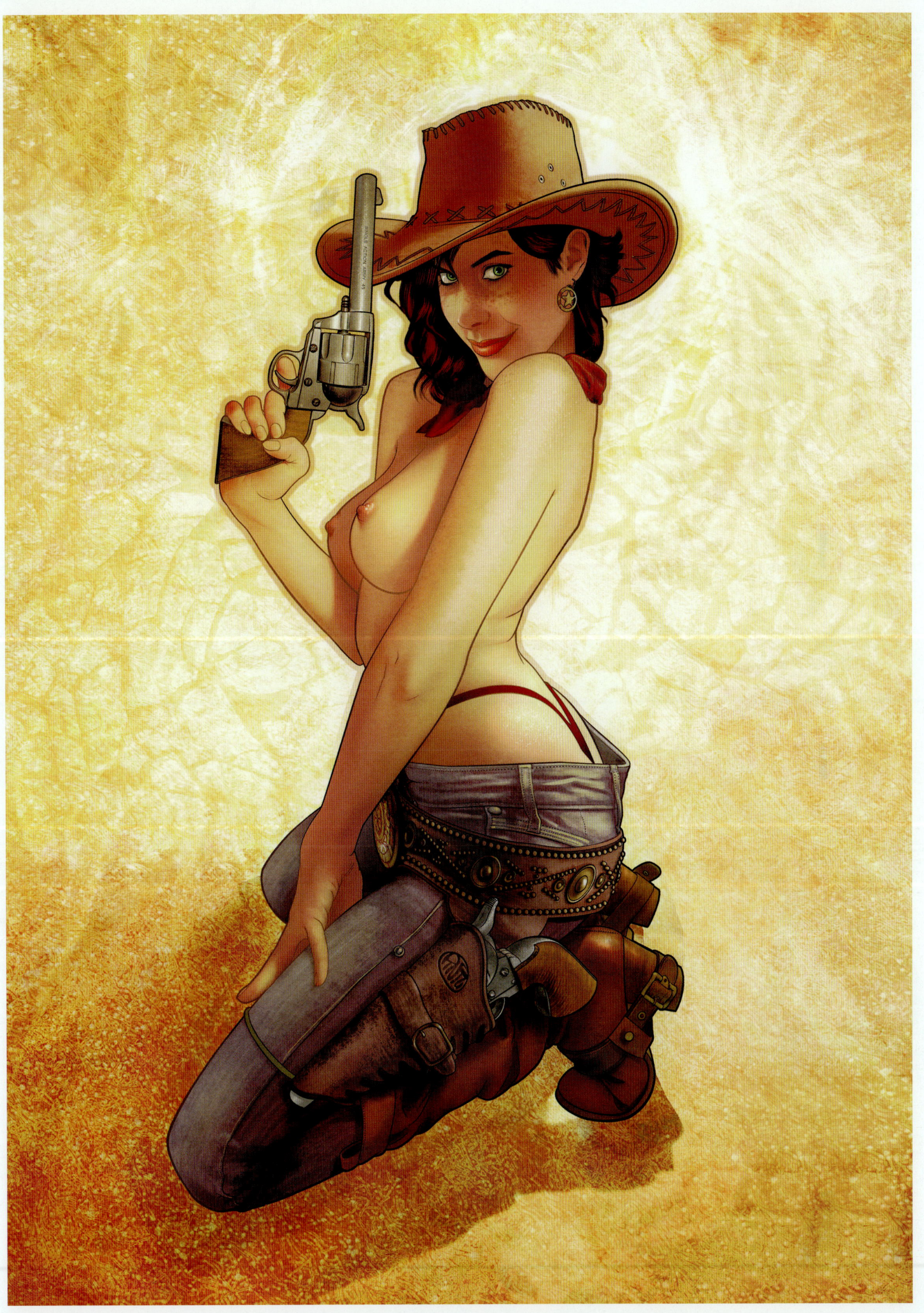

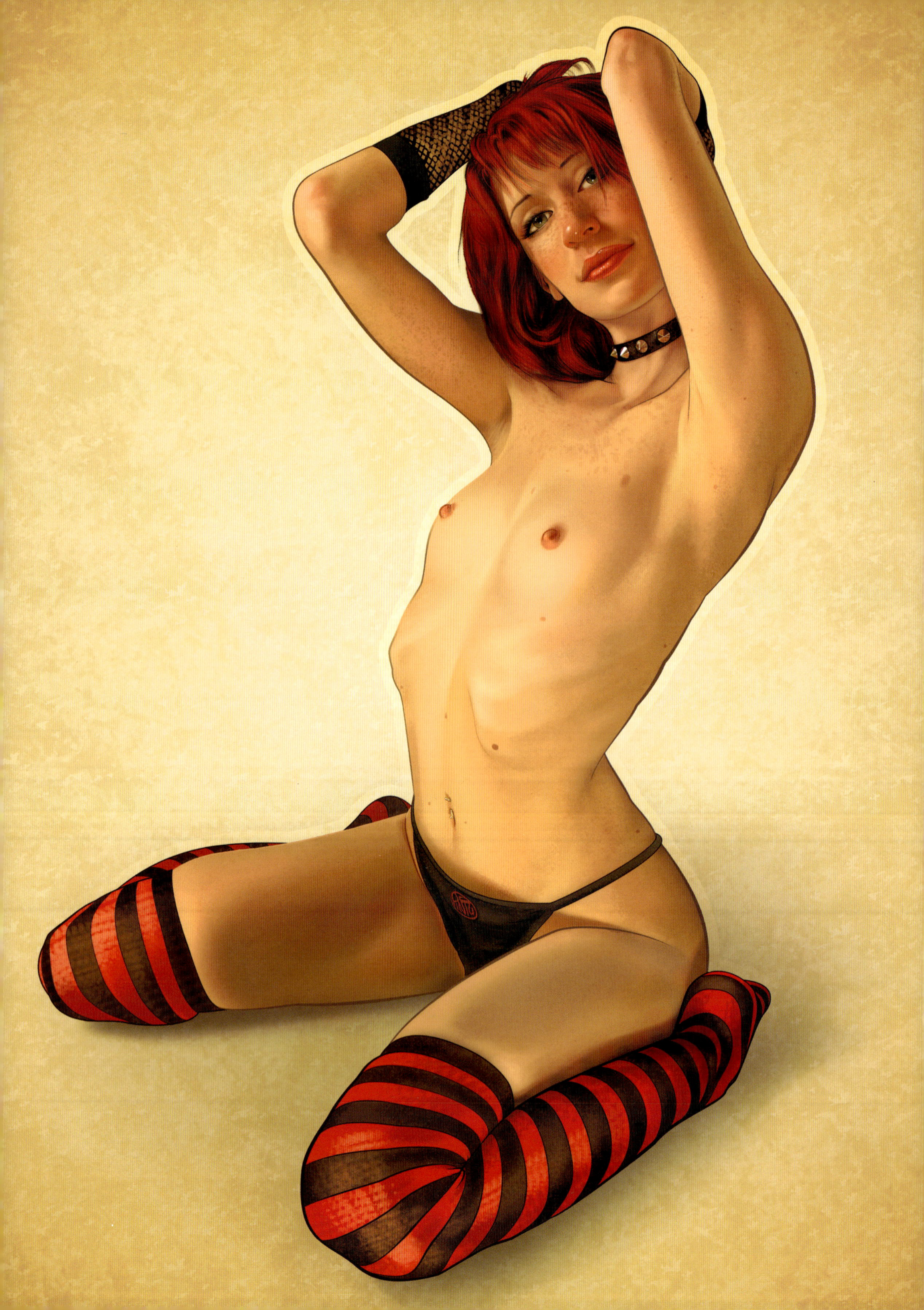

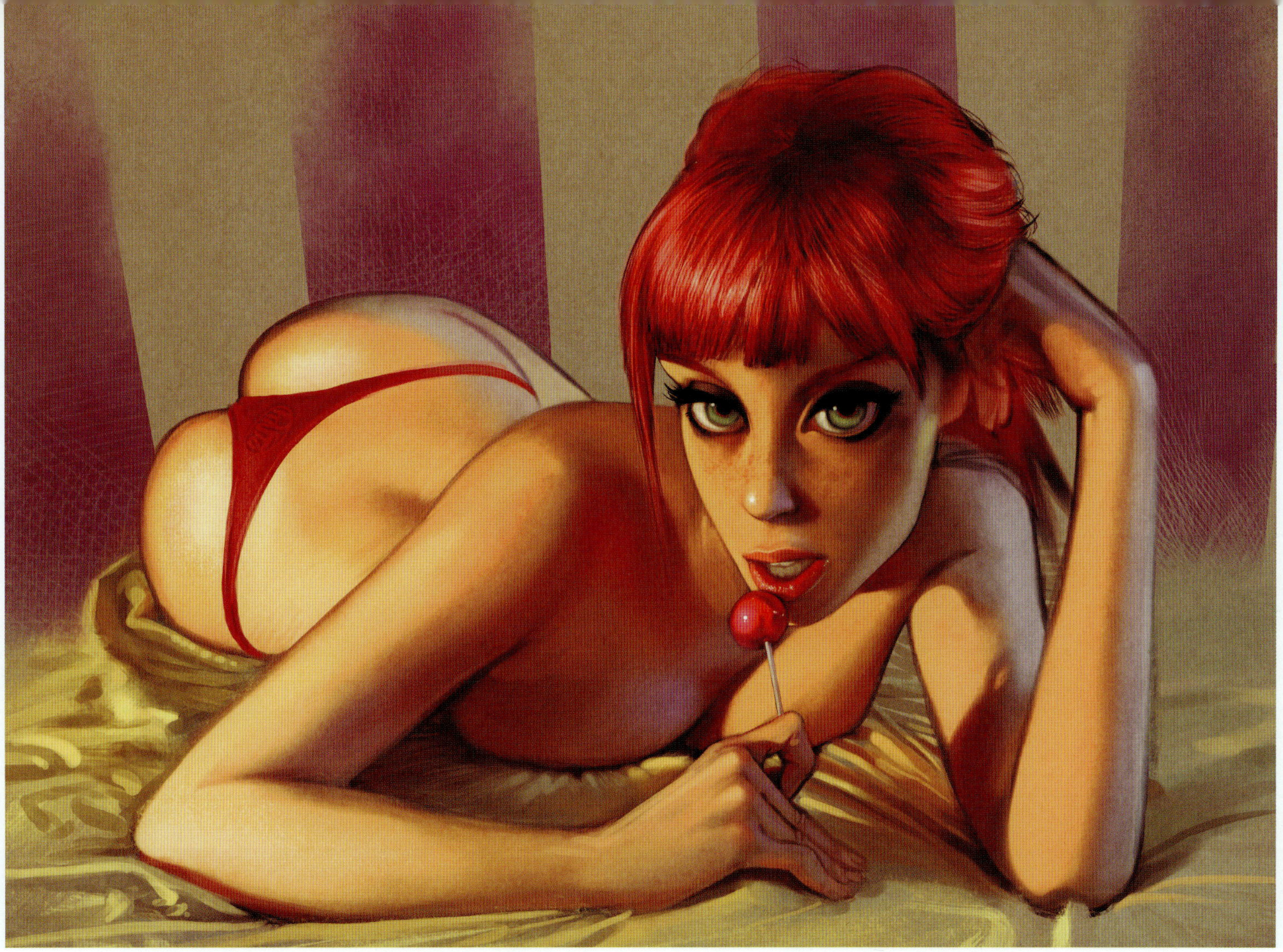

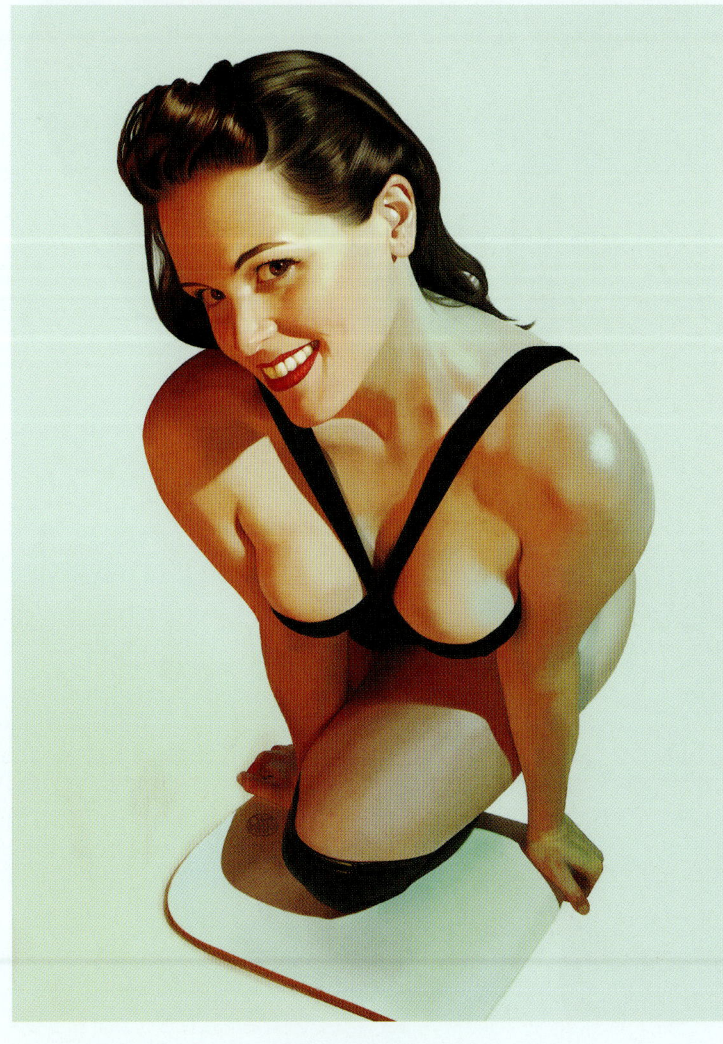

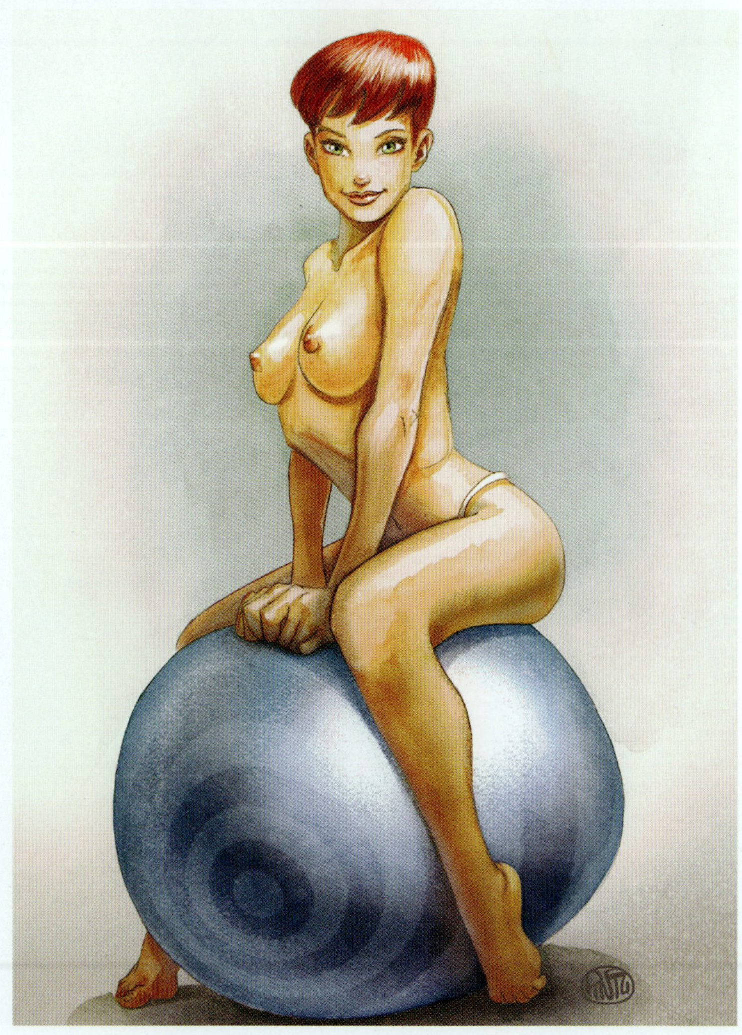

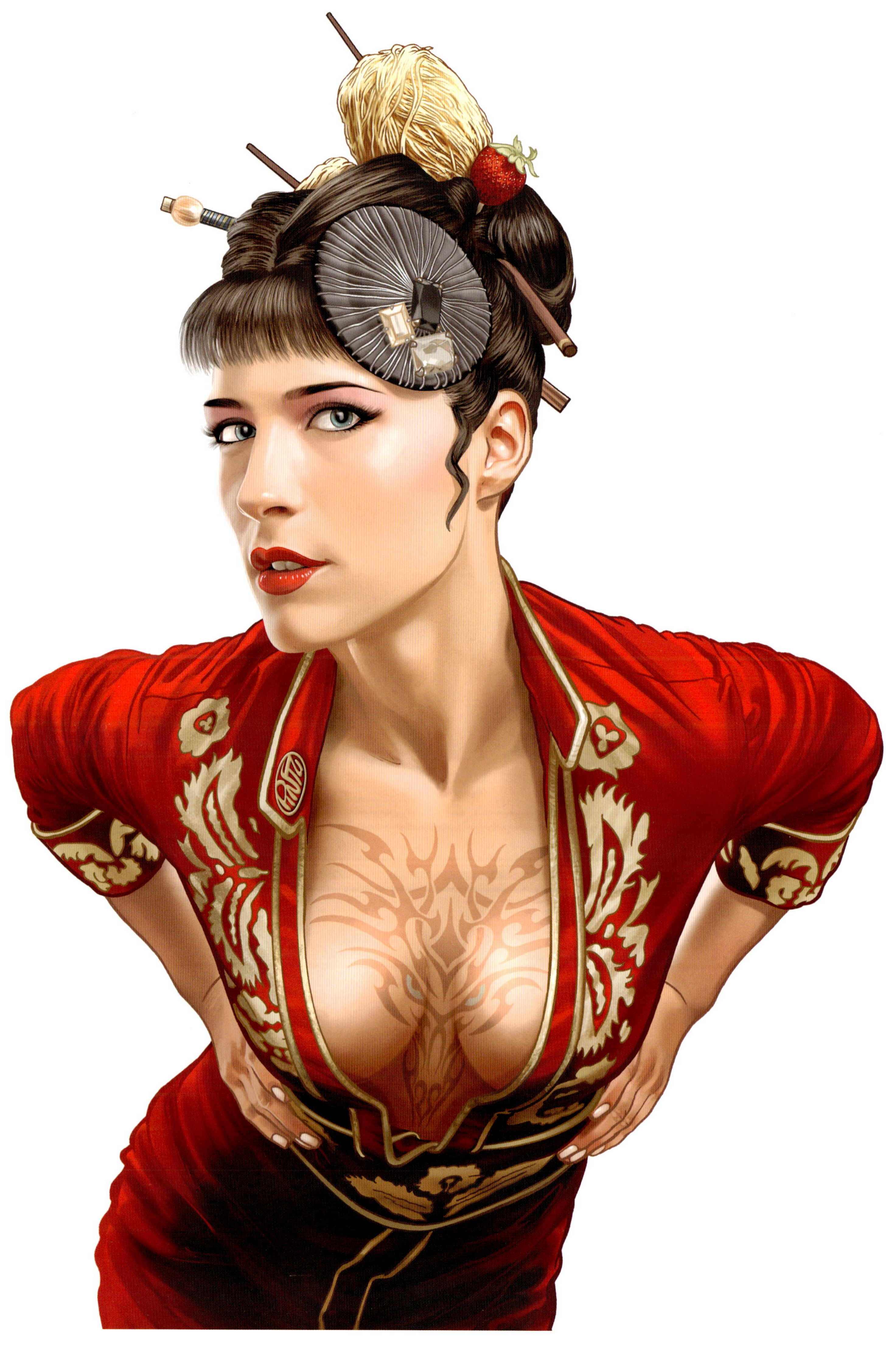

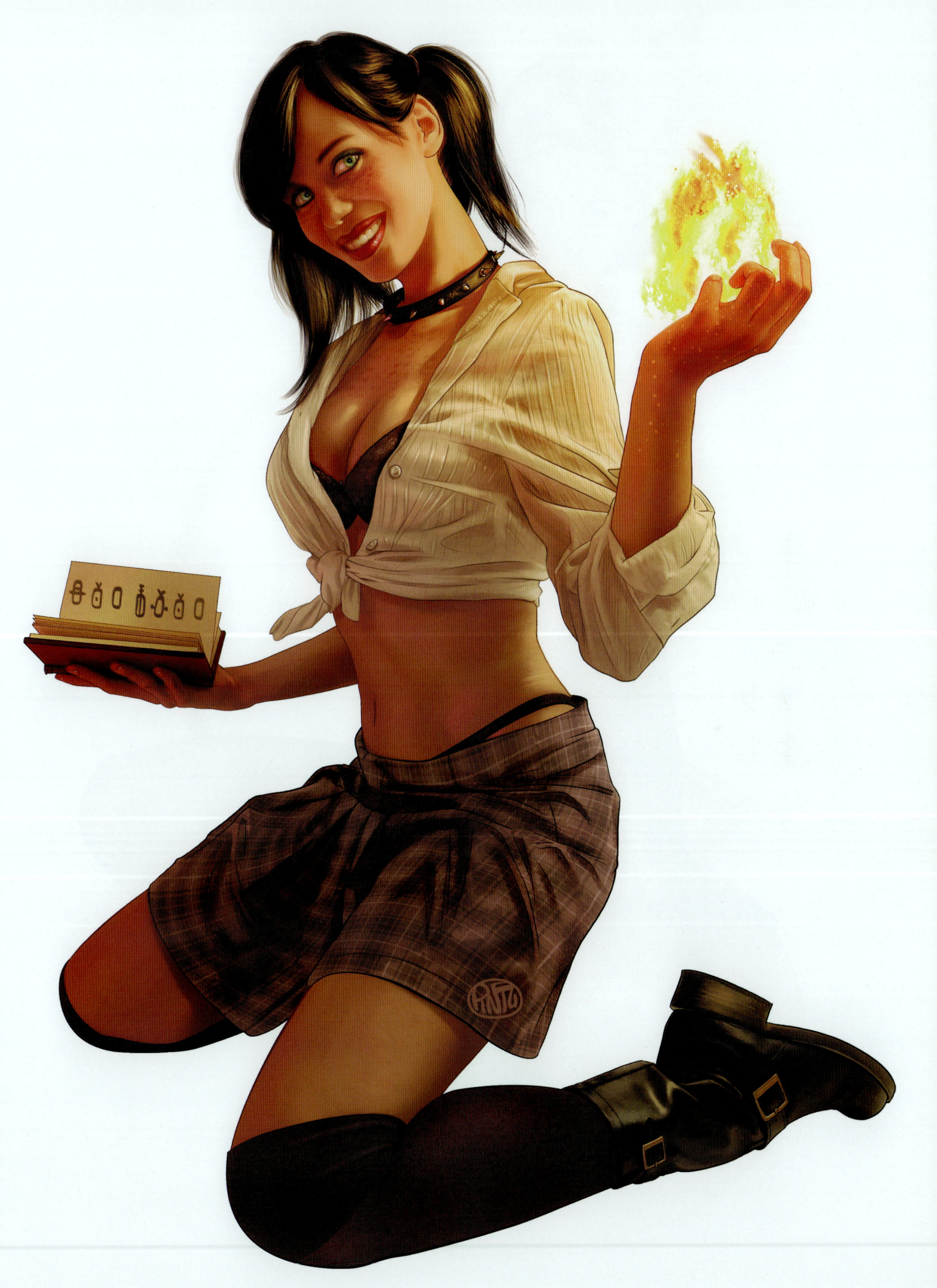

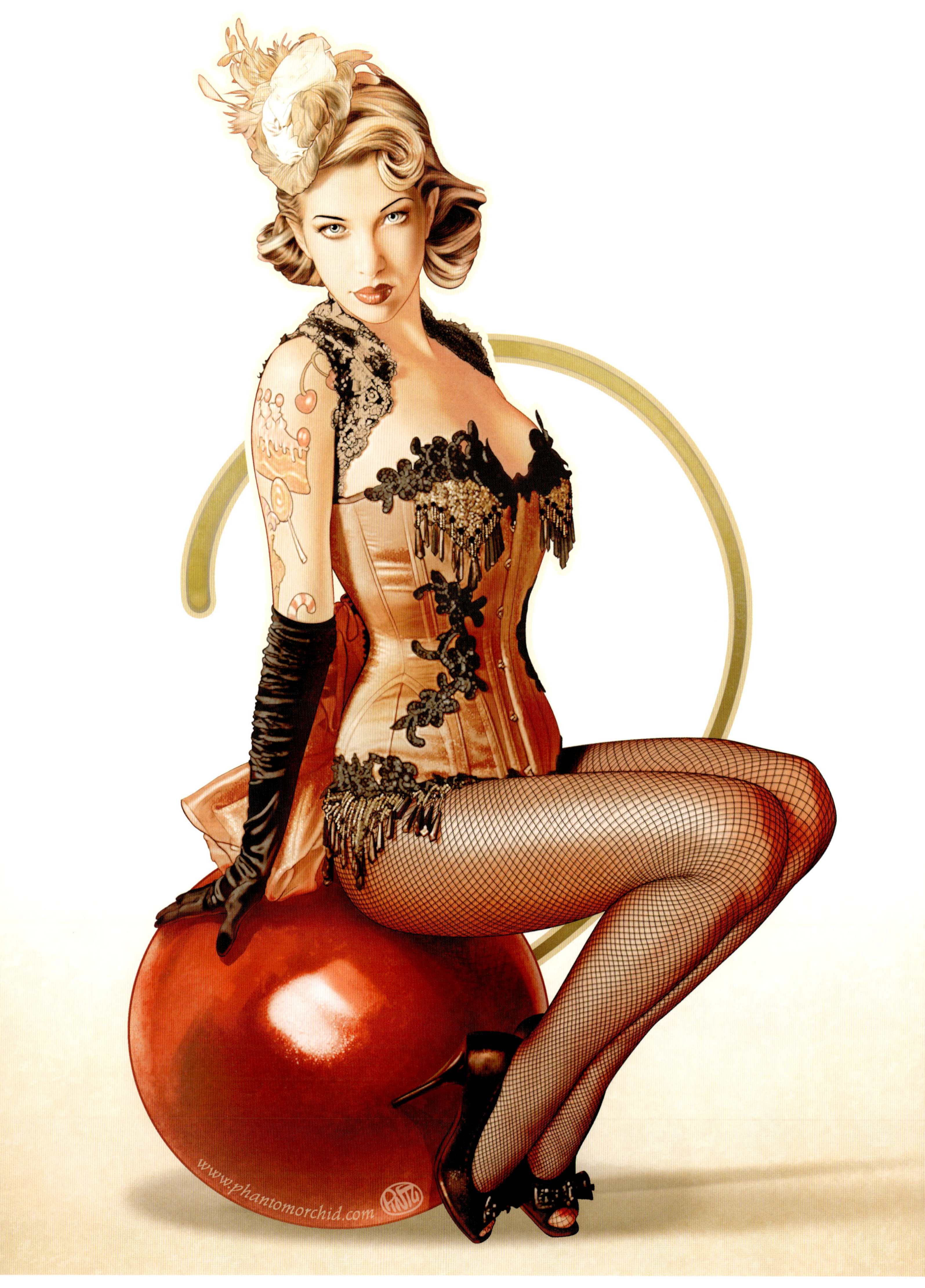
www.phantomorchid.com

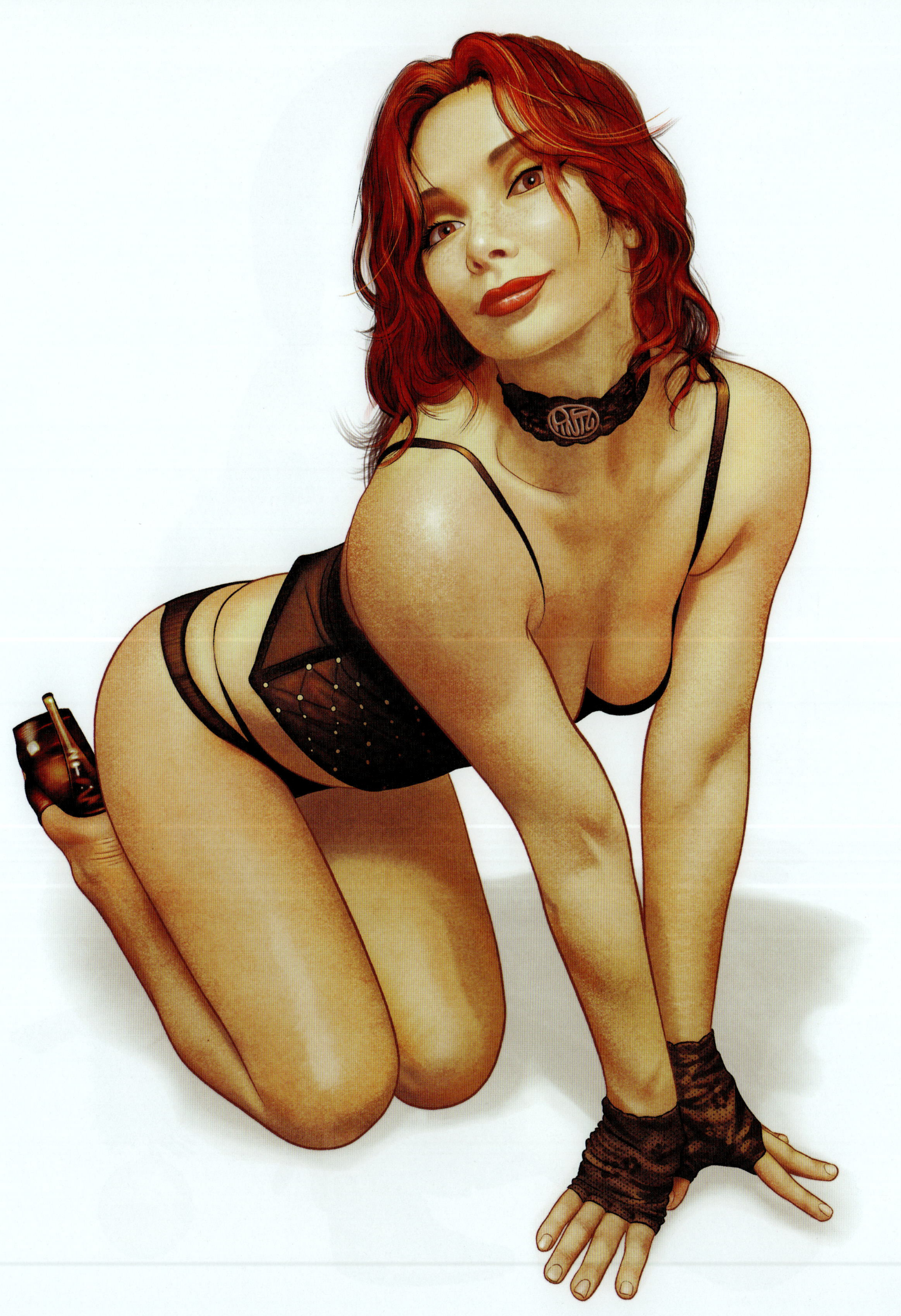

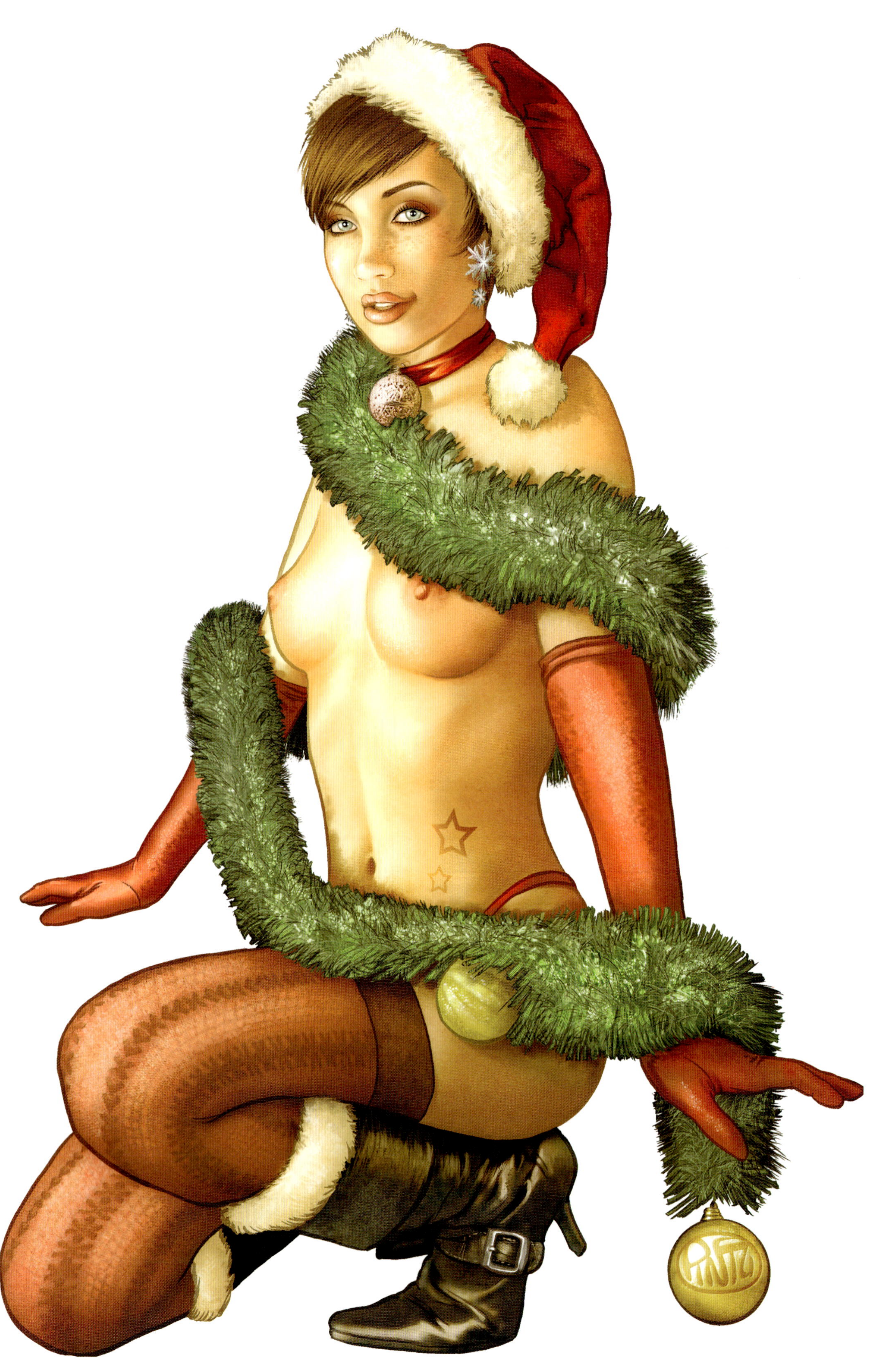

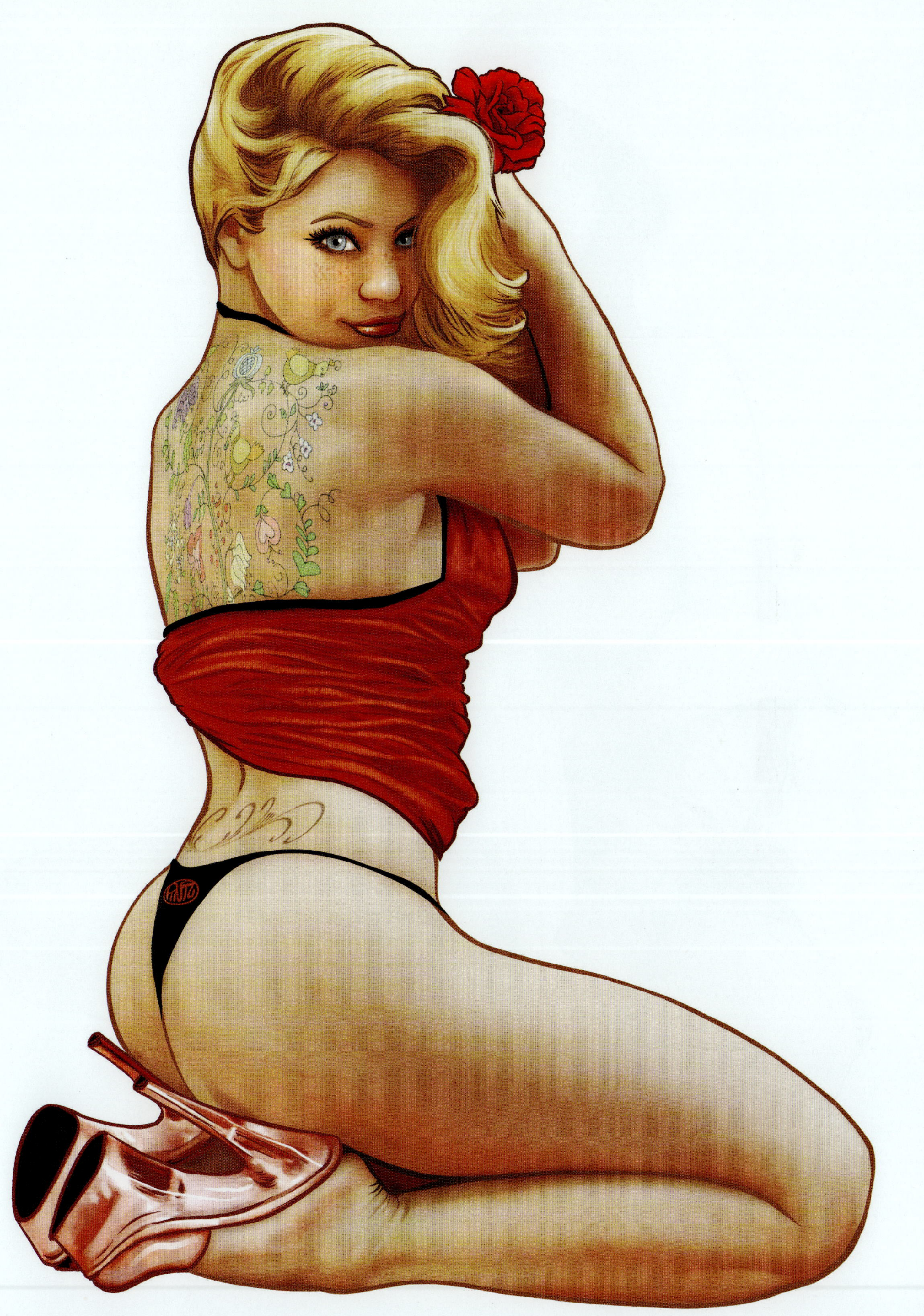

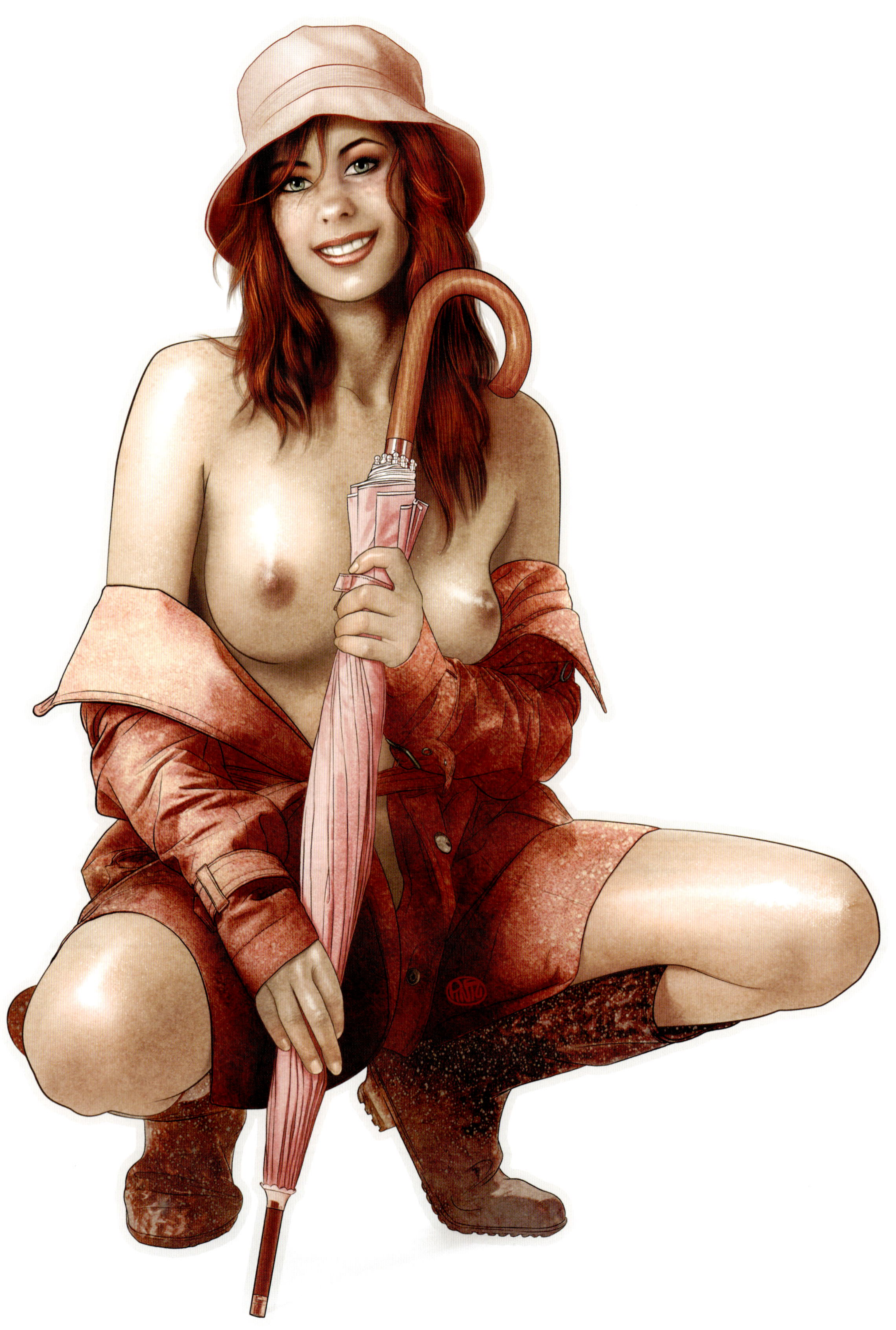

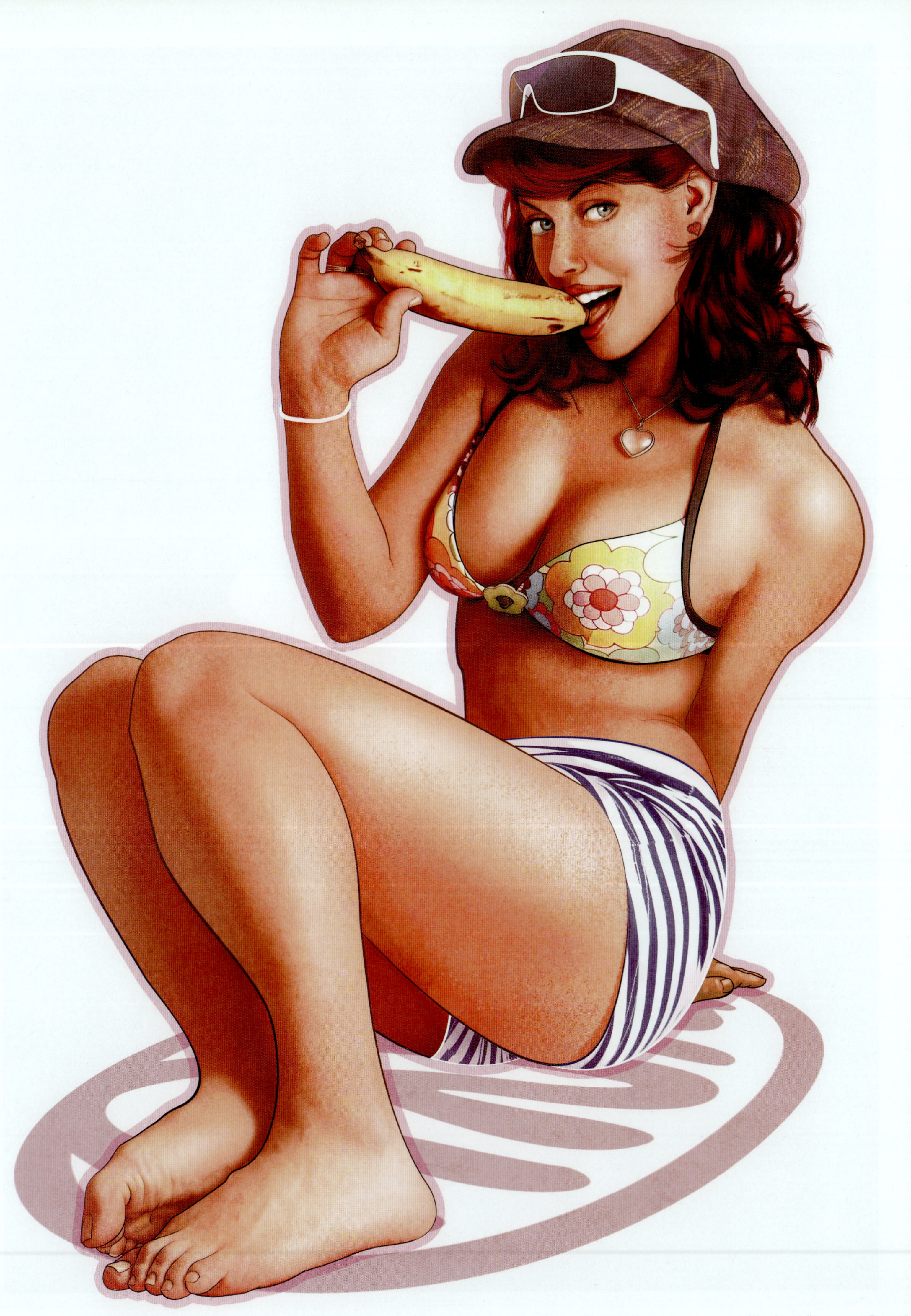

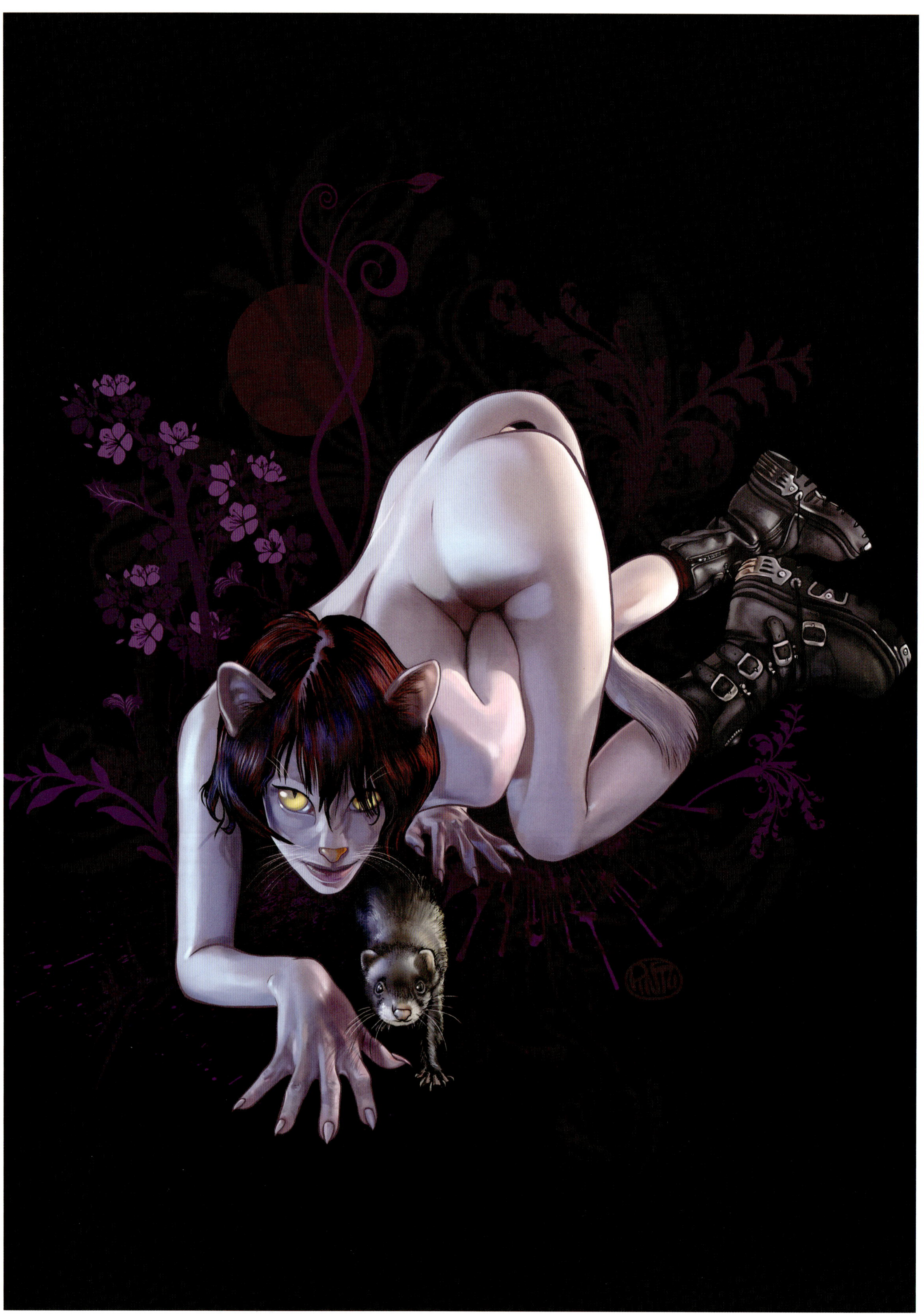

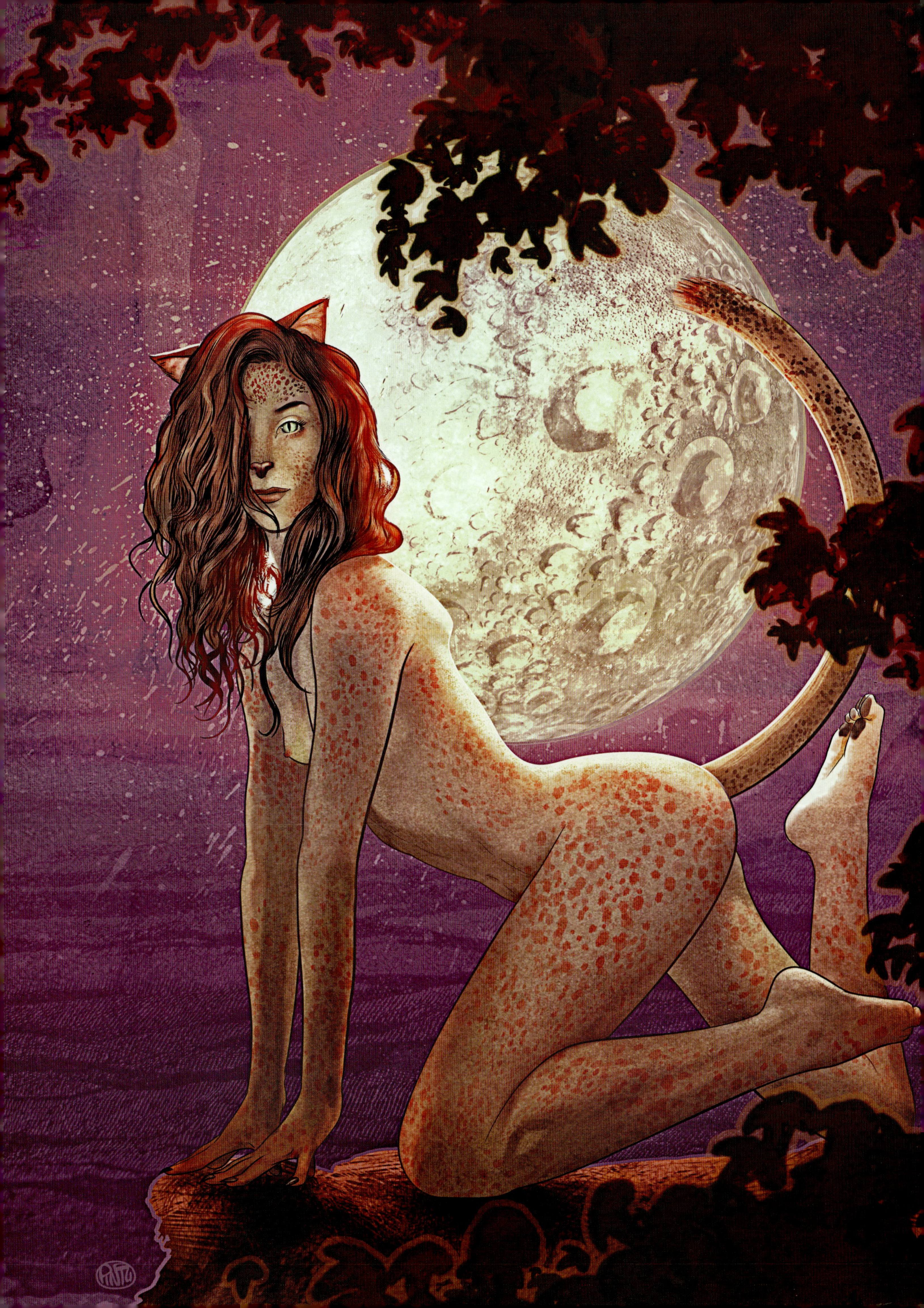

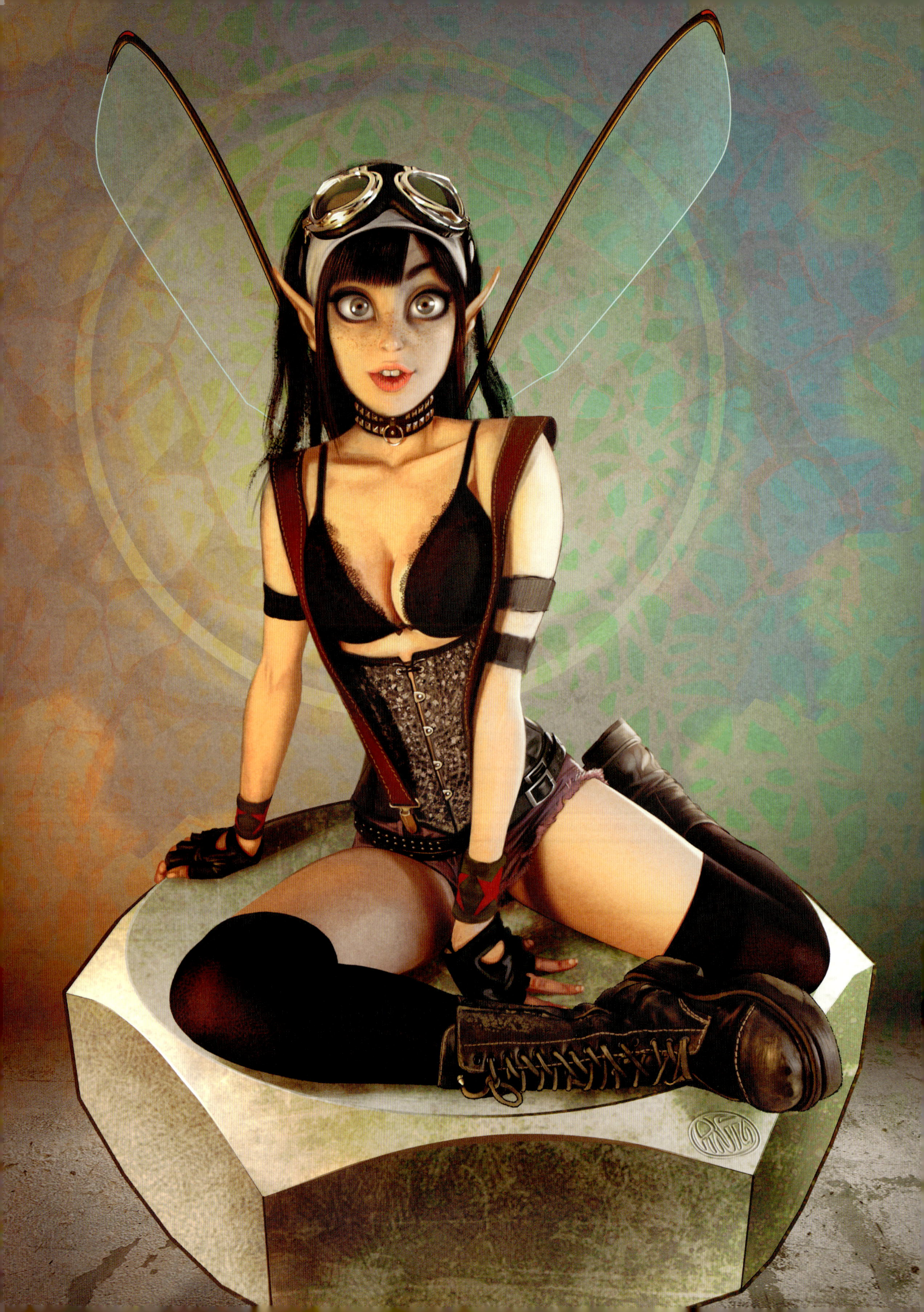

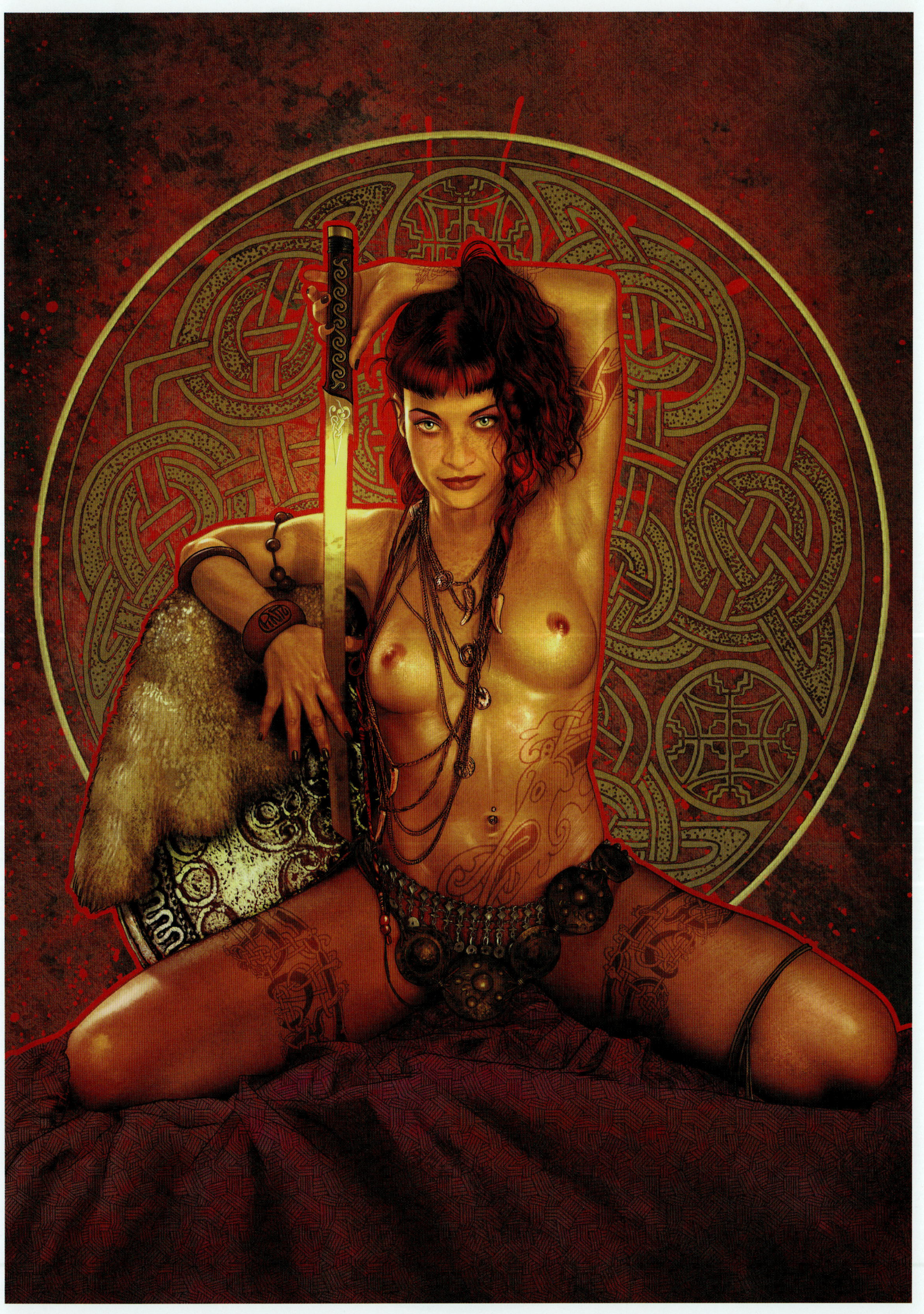

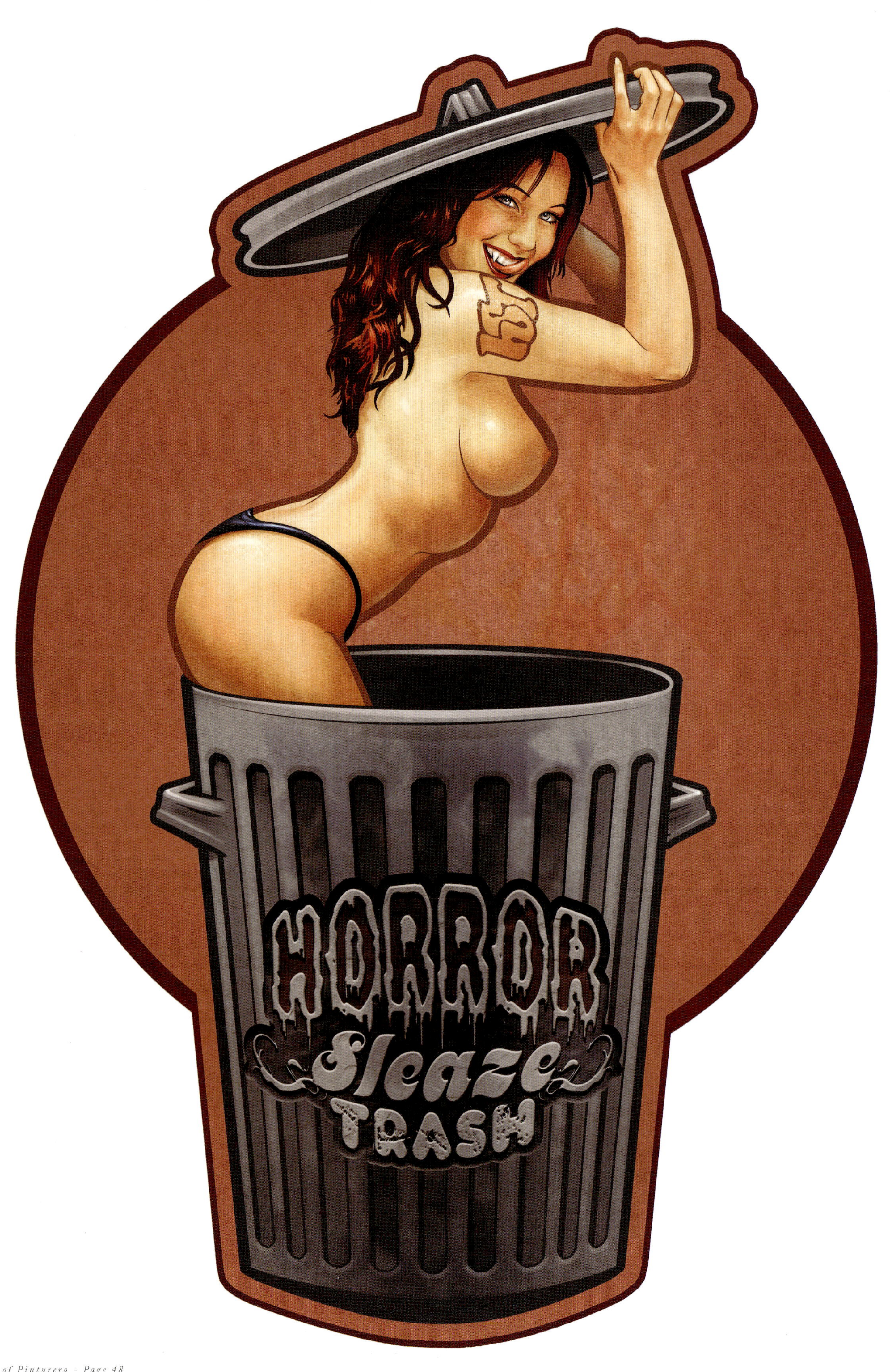
HORROR
Sleaze
TRASH